CELEBRITY
SERVICE

GEOFF RAMM

ISBN 978-1-912300-37-2

Published in 2021 by SRA Books

A CIP record of this book is available from the British Library.

Text design by Nick Redeyoff
Photograph of Geoff Ramm by Ian West
Typeset in 11pt Sabon
Printed in the UK

WHAT THEY SAY ABOUT CELEBRITY SERVICE

'Geoff has the ability to capture, engage and motivate his audience. He brings you into the room and keeps you with him. He has a lively and entertaining style that leaves you wanting more! The engagement comes from the stories that are real life and relatable. Some very astute and intelligent observations from all walks of life that translate into great tools to help guide teams. The magic is in the title. Who doesn't want to be a celebrity?!

I have been living and breathing Geoff's mantra for many years with significant success, enabling consecutive years of growth. He gets it and is great fun to work with.'

Ed Bracken, General Manager, Crowne Plaza, The City, London

Talk about WOW! Geoff can light up a room, inspire innovative thoughts, and ignite a desire to be the most talked about business on *Earth*. He has people second guessing their most awesome service experience, wondering when the next Hollywood or A-list celebrity will come waltzing in, and thinking about how to fill the "Celebrity Service gap" in a split second.

All with positive energy and a sense of purpose. Geoff Ramm will help you *see* the difference and *be* the difference!'

Olivia Sarah-Le Lacheur, General Manager, Retail Distribution – Partnership Development, AIA/CommInsure

Geoff's passion, energy and enthusiasm shines as brightly the first time you meet him as it does when he takes to the stage, immediately capturing the audience and holding them for the whole set. He had the post-lunch graveyard shift buzzing from the off.

At first glance you might think that the Celebrity Service philosophy and Geoff's examples bear no relation to your business, but you'd be wrong. Celebrity Service can help anyone build stronger relationships with their customers; his approach and the tools he uses are easy to understand, adapt and implement.'

Graham Thorley, Head of Communications, Balfour Beatty, UK Construction Services

Geoff Ramm has a uniquely engaging style that appeals to all ages, and all stages of people's careers. Without doubt, the two sessions that he has held for us have reshaped our strategy on client engagement and client satisfaction – leading to us running our own "Celebrity Service" programme. The phrase "What would Geoff do?" is frequently heard in our office.

So pleased are we with the long term effect of what Geoff has had to say that we have asked him to be our keynote speaker at our international conference next year for Mackrell International, where we will have international lawyers from up to 60 countries gathered in London – evidence that his expertise has no global boundaries.'

Nigel Rowley, Managing Partner, Head of International, Past Chairman of Mackrell International

Geoff is one of the most engaging speakers I have ever worked with, his energy and enthusiasm is infectious. His knowledge and insight into customer service and marketing is both entertaining and thought-provoking, both of which assist in reshaping the way we think. Celebrity Service is a perfect way to illustrate where the gap is when delivering customer service. Geoff and his Celebrity Service philosophy has been hugely instrumental in guiding us through our thought process when reviewing our customer experience.

His delivery is both engaging and humorous and has a long lasting effect on his audience.'

Heather McNamee, Area General Manager,
Frasers Hospitality UK Ltd

Geoff has an infectious enthusiasm that allows you to travel the journey with him sharing insights into not only what makes a service experience memorable but to also share how that feels as the recipient. I did not feel I was in the audience, but rather that I was alongside him living the content. Audiences are not only uplifted and motivated, they leave with new insights and easy to implement take-aways.

Geoff's Celebrity Service is all about taking the extra steps with consideration, creativity and awesomeness to deliver an outcome that changes a person's perspective, expectations and reality. To deliver Celebrity Service is to deliver delight, going beyond the normal with simple gifts of thought and care that result in a smile and sense of appreciation that last a lifetime. Celebrity Service is delivering that special magic that people just want to share.'

Susan Paterson, Director & Authorised Representative, B I G
Financial Services & MDRT

Geoff delivered an energised and entertaining session on Celebrity Service to the audience at Business Network Live, Wella's annual two-day business-focussed, residential event for salon owners and managers from across the hairdressing industry. His plenary was fast paced and insightful, Geoff gave some thought-provoking observations to highlight key content points and his engagement with the audience was spot on. Our audience loved Geoff's delivery and we look forward to welcoming him back to deliver "OMG Marketing".

The Celebrity Service philosophy ideas and techniques delivered were perfect for the audience, providing them with multiple ideas, giving them the edge over their competition. There was some great actionable content and examples that were relevant to business of all sizes, as well as clear direction on how to engage the salons' teams to support for the best results.'

Allie Hargreaves, Education and Events Operations Manager, Wella Professional UKI

Original content that brings real results! Geoff is a highly engaging speaker. He was hugely enthusiastic about our business, inspiring all our team to introduce new ideas across the dealerships based on the Celebrity Service concept.'

James Richardson, General Manager, Service, Suzuki GB PLC

Geoff is one of the most engaging and energising speakers I've come across in recent times, he challenges you to think beyond the ordinary and brings Celebrity Service to life with relevant examples and a smattering of humour.

The Celebrity Service philosophy is simple, take what you think is pretty good service and think, "How can I make it extraordinary?", but only Geoff Ramm has the skill to help you find that new horizon.'

Philip Kewin, Chief Executive Officer, Association of Financial Advisers Ltd

ABOUT
GEOFF

Like you, Geoff Ramm, the creator of Celebrity Service, knows that great customer service leads to lucrative repeat business. On the other hand, a greater experience leads to global recognition.

So how can you design a customer experience that has you talked about for decades to come?

Geoff knows the Jedi mind trick to make you craved by your customers, envied by your competitors and raved about in your industry.

In this book and through his interactive keynotes, your teams and audience will not only discover out-of-this-world ideas, they will come up with their own and be excited to implement them too.

He has challenged and inspired entrepreneurs, companies and organisations across six continents to create award-winning ideas to outperform the competition.

He still loves his pizza, he still loves his cider and (unfortunately) he still loves his beloved club, Sunderland.

'A game changer.' *Forbes*.

CONTENTS

This book is dedicated to my very own Superstars.

Firstly, my loving, efficient and courageous wife Hayley.

Also my incredibly creative daughter Grace and my energy-filled son Elliot.

Let nothing stop you from achieving the dreams you have today.

BEFORE WE GET STARTED...

What you are about to read is not a customer experience strategic blueprint. If you love graphs, charts, figures and analytics please look away now. However, if you are ready to embark on a global tour of amazing people, doing amazing things, delivering wonderful experiences then you are in the right place.

I must also forewarn you that you are about to come across quite a few stories relating to *Star Wars*. It wasn't intentional. It just happened. Honest. If this is okay with you then this is definitely the book you've been looking for.

You will notice that a lot of my observations occur while I am away with family or working with clients. I seem to find the very best examples of Celebrity Service Superstars when on holiday, staying in hotels, visiting attractions or simply speaking to clients and audiences in corridors.

I am often asked where I get my stories and ideas from. My answer is simply, 'Just leave the house. They are everywhere!'

The interviews in the book are with people I've worked with throughout the years. One of the best parts of being in business is the people you meet along your journey who go on to become close business friends.

So with the disclaimers and admissions out of the way we can now concentrate on how you and your team can become Celebrity Service Superstars.

What is it that Superstars do? (see page 19)? What can you learn from them? And how can you adapt their thinking into your own business, ensuring a greater service experience for both you, your team and your customers.

Within this book you will discover the simple, easy and yet cost-effective ways in which you can make a huge difference to your customer's experience.

You will take away insights and nuggets from the Superstar interviews.

You will once again delve into the award-winning 120 Challenge interactive technique to generate fresh and inspiring ideas for your own business.

You will also read some of my most recent stories, drawn from my travels from Dublin to Dubai, Sydney to Sunderland and Texas to Truro.

So, without further ado, let's hit the Celebrity Service Superstar highway!

LA STORY

The dream begins...

Back in the 1980s, television sets across the UK were about to be hit hard. Giants covered in war paint were set to raid our screens, stealing viewing figures. Yes, American football was arriving in our living rooms, bringing with it fireworks, half-time shows, cheerleaders and a feast of stars the like we had not seen on our 4:3 screens.

Until then, the fridge was something we kept our cream soda, limeade and Irn-Bru in. Now The Fridge was a 6 foot 2 inch 335 lb superstar who played for the Chicago Bears, one of the teams that transcended the sport across the Atlantic Ocean.

This type of football was a far cry from the football I'd known standing in the Fulwell End terrace of Roker Park with a rolled-up programme in my back pocket, eating a boiled burger with soggy onions.

This explosion of colour, glitz, glam, funky names, uniforms and stadia. This was something else altogether.

Yes, I fell in love with football. American football.

I wasn't the only child in Whitburn junior school to witness the spectacle that was the NFL – the National Football League. A few of my fellow classmates were also hooked from the very first snap.

Now where could we buy an American football to play in the school yard? We couldn't. Amazon was still three decades away. So we used a nearby branch and chucked it for all it was worth until the bell rang.

Having watched for a few weeks, it was time to pick a team to support. Who would you follow? Which teams appealed? I picked the Los Angeles Raiders. I loved their badge, with its silver and black. And I loved their passionate fans, who were reminiscent of my own home football team of Sunderland. For good measure I also chose the Los Angeles Rams as my second team (for some reason I was drawn to the name).

Both teams played their home games at the iconic Coliseum. It's a stadium I remember fondly from watching the 1984 Summer Olympic Games. Carl Lewis, Ed Moses, Lord Sebastian Coe, Tessa Sanderson, Daley Thompson and of course the Jarrow Arrow himself, Steve Cram. Oh and the more-than-charismatic 400-metre specialist Kriss Akabusi who I'd later work alongside at a conference in Malta. Surreal.

As the seasons passed I'd often say to myself…

One day…

One day… I'll go there.

Los Angeles…

Celebrity and the Hollywood Hills

The Celebrity Service keynote talks, the interactive group sessions and the original book have all delivered incredibly successful results. Delivering the philosophy and sharing the inspiring stories around the world, audiences from CEOs to people on day-release from college just get it. They get its simplicity. They understand how it can be adopted into their own business culture. And I am extremely proud of that.

But the brand itself is of course an adaptation of the Hollywood Hills. And the subsequent nine stages of CELEBRITY (Consistency, Excitement, Love, Engagement, Bravado, Response, Independence, Thank You, You and Your Team) are also creative designs based on one of the most iconic structures in the world.

One day I'll go there…

Los Angeles…

At the time of writing I have spoken in 44 separate countries and have visited and spoken in some of the most amazing places. From Tehran to Kyoto, from Oslo to Cape Town, Tallinn to Auckland, Sydney to South Shields. Each time I travel to a conference I pinch myself. To step through the places I'd only ever seen paraded as quiz show star prizes has and always will be a wonderful part of my business life. South Shields exempt.

Then… it happened…

The enquiry came in… oh boy…

The contract was signed… my, oh my…

I was going to…

Los Angeles.

Boarding swiftly

It was now time to fly to the destination that I had been dreaming of since childhood.

I boarded the Aer Lingus flight from Dublin to Los Angeles. I'd just watched England beat Panama 6-1 in the World Cup group match in the departure lounge so I was naturally on a high. To add to my happiness the Irish airline proceeded to serve Magners cider on board. Could it get any better? Well, yes actually, it could.

I secured my hand luggage, took my seat and buckled up. The gentleman across the aisle said hello and shook my hand introducing himself as James. He was sat next to his daughter Nadine who was coming home after a very serious car accident. Somewhere over the Atlantic Ocean I found out she was Taylor Swift's lead dancer on her world tour. Despite her evident discomfort we spoke at length and she signed my boarding card for Grace.

Cider (me) and whisky (James) in hand we chatted for a solid nine hours. We talked about business, the conference I was appearing at, travel, family and of course… American football. I also shared with James the dream I'd had since watching that Channel 4 footage back in the 1980s. The flight literally flashed past.

The seat belt sign pinged. Empty Magners glass returned, the wheels touched down. I was on Californian tarmac.

One day I'll go…

I'm there!

I messaged Hayley with my signature arrivals message 'Touchdown… LA'.

Twenty-four hours later the phone rang in my hotel room.
The concierge informed me there was a parcel waiting in reception.
I imagined it was a welcome pack from the event organisers. So I
took the lift down. It was a large brown padded bag and it was soft.
I tore the end and pulled out a black and silver Raiders jersey, with a
message attached from James wishing me a great event. Wow!
He remembered our chat. My dream. The hotel I was staying in.
He remembered. He thought. He actioned.

Welcome to the land of Celebrity Service.

I had a couple of days before my talk during which I had two goals.
One was to adjust my body clock and two, to see some of that
tinseltown stuff – namely the stadium, the Hollywood sign and of
course, to walk along the boulevard of stars. I met a gentleman
called Mark Bertie on the bus tour, a fellow Brit who told me his
wife Theresa was also attending the very same conference. We
became Brit travel buddies as we explored Hollywood together.

The Hollywood sign is just one of those things you see on television.
And you literally have to scrunch up and adjust your eyes multiple
times to take it all in. It's just letters on a hillside to most, but to
me it was honestly one of those moments that I found difficult to
take in. Mark and I got really close to it and while we were taking
photographs and watching out for snakes (there were warning signs
dotted all around) we were suddenly surrounded by a hundred police
officers. We hadn't strayed into a no-go zone or anything like that.
They were involved in a publicity photoshoot. As we spoke to them I
noticed even their vehicles were displaying signs of Celebrity Service.

We then travelled to the home of the LA Rams, the Coliseum.
We couldn't set foot in the stadium itself due to off-season building
work taking place. But it didn't really matter. I was there. I had the
selfie to prove it.

I was at the previous home of my favourite Stars 'n' Stripes team.
(They moved back to Oakland and are now based in Las Vegas.)

After seeing the buildings used in *Lethal Weapon* and the walkways
and stores of *Pretty Woman* we went to search for the famous names
along the star-studded Hollywood Boulevard. It takes a while to
step across 2500 five-pointed terrazzo and brass stars embedded in
the pavements across 15 blocks, but we managed. With the phone
switched to camera mode, I had my head down, taking in the who's
who of film, stage, music and television. And my favourite was…

The stars

These iconic names placed on the ground mean so much to so many people. Exploring them takes you back to childhood memories of your favourite movies.

The stars who are there all achieved something. They have written the scripts, delivered legendary performances, they have made us laugh as well as cry, they have entertained us and they are part of our culture. Visiting them in this way... I loved it!

These are the people on Hollywood Boulevard. Those who have done amazing things; those who have inspired; those who have entertained; those who have achieved fame. They have done something in their lives and have been recognised.

In this book, the follow up to *Celebrity Service*, I wanted to find out more about the Celebrity Service stars on the street. I wanted to come down from the philosophy of the hills and move closer to the stars of the show. I wanted to dig deeper. I wanted to interview the stars I have come across in my work and in my travels.

What have they done? How have they achieved success? Why do they do what they do? What ignites them into delivering an incredible experience? What drives their passion for service? What are their own personal experiences? What are the things that drive them crazy and the things they'd do differently if they had a magic wand?

I hope that their ideas, the culture and their ways of thinking will help to inspire you and your business to continually create a greater Celebrity Service experience.

Of course, I'll also be sharing some of my latest stories about Celebrity Service along the way.

First and foremost, this book is focused on the stars themselves.

Let the lion roar.

Let the curtain rise.

Let the spotlight shine.

Let the show begin.

WHAT MAKES A CELEBRITY SERVICE SUPERSTAR?

- ★ They have heart
- ★ They have character
- ★ They give back
- ★ They spot opportunities
- ★ They take action
- ★ They do what is right in the moment
- ★ They smile through gritted teeth
- ★ They laugh
- ★ They don't set rules
- ★ They'll turn a blind eye for the benefit of you
- ★ They do what others fail to see
- ★ They cut red tape
- ★ They open the door for you

★ They replace what's broken (even when it's not their fault)

★ They call you back

★ They give you their extension number

★ They kneel down to talk to small children

★ They don't leave you on hold to listen to the entire back catalogue of Beethoven

★ They respond quicker than you'd imagine

★ They arrive earlier

★ They stay later

★ They let you off with it when you are 1p over at the petrol station

★ They don't pull the shutters down 10 minutes before they close

★ They wrap your gift

★ They compliment

★ They take their own coat off and give it to you

★ They put a little extra in your order

★ They walk out holding the umbrella

★ They appreciate your business

★ They tell you they appreciate your business

★ They don't use templates

ONE FOR THE TEAM

Before you commit to delivering it to external customers, remember that Celebrity Service starts at home, in your workplace. It starts with your colleagues, your team and your workforce. Here are two of my favourite examples of internal Celebrity Service.

Hullywood service

I set the alarm earlier than normal and said my goodbyes to the fantastic team at voco™ St David's Hotel in Cardiff.

I was on a mission. A surprise mission.

I made my way eight miles south-west to a place called Barry Island. The home of Stacey, Bryn, Nessa, Pam and the wonderful stars of the British hit sitcom *Gavin & Stacey*. Yes my wife Hayley and I are big fans, but so too is our daughter Grace. So I wanted to get there early to surprise her. As I got to Barry, Grace was travelling to school. I Facetimed her, flipped the video and spun around to show the fairground and the famous bus stop. With Grace on my phone, I walked along the beach, imagining James Corden still licking an ice cream in the background. These are iconic locations for fans of the show, shared, as they are, with dog walkers of a morning.

Big smiles shone through the phone before we said our goodbyes and Grace headed through the school gates. Surprise accomplished. A quick coffee in Marco's, then kicking off the sand from my shoes, I was ready for a 5-hour cross-country drive to the east coast of Yorkshire – to Hull.

I was due to arrive at the Bonus Arena that afternoon to run through my slides and do a sound check. My client, a famous British brand Swift, design, manufacture and supply amazing vehicles and products all over the world. At some point in your life (especially if you live in the UK) there is a huge chance you or your family will have stayed in one of their caravans or motorhomes. If not, you'll certainly have overtaken one or two on the motorway.

It had been at the dealership conference the previous summer where we had first worked together. Amy Archer and Beth Rookes delivered a wonderful event for their UK dealership network and days later they'd re-booked me – this time to deliver for their entire workforce of just over 1000 in Hull.

Before the company-wide event, I was keen to explore and experience their culture and to see how they designed and created the products I remembered so well from childhood. So they invited me down to tour the plant and to meet some of the team. It was a brilliant experience: from the design room, to the cutting of the materials, to the lines of skilled workers expertly piecing together every section. Watching two sides of a caravan being lifted together and then fixed into place was very impressive. However, what truly shone out that day was the pride, passion and devotion in the eyes and the words of every Swift team member. It was inspiring to see.

Back to the Bonus Arena and the sound and slide check. I met Amy and the team once again and as the mic was being clipped to my lapel she asked, 'I hope you like the ideas we have planned to open the conference?' I turned round to face the stage, where there were a dozen dancers primed to begin rehearsing. And then the music kicked in. First of all a booming 1960s hit to which the dancers matched the sounds of that decade with their moves. Followed by tunes and dances from the 1970s, 1980s, 1990s and so on, right up to the current day. Add to this, flame-wielding sticks lighting up the stage as The Prodigy's *Firestarter* boomed out.

But the best was still to come…

Behind the onstage show was a giant screen. This is where the Celebrity Service experience would be delivered to every team member.

The marketing team had collated the names of every Swift employee (over 1000) and listed them in order of the day they started work for the company. As the choreographed performances moved through the decades, each colleague's name, together with the year they began working at Swift, was flashed up on the screen.

Never in my conference speaking career have I seen such fine detail to welcome the audience into an auditorium. Forget your tote bags, miniature giveaways, vouchers and stress balls. Give your team recognition. Put them on the big screen. Put them all on the big screen!

I was over the moon when Amy added a bonus for me on top of this lovely experience. Having heard me share my Moneypenny story at their summer dealership conference (it's in the first *Celebrity Service* book), she told me they had all gone back to the office to create their very own 120 Challenge (see page 59). The aim was to help them create a Celebrity Service moment for the entire team. And that's where the 'names on the screen' idea was born.

A day later, standing at the front of the conference hall I looked across a sea of beaming smiles as the team spotted their names and the date they started.

Whether you decide to set your alarm earlier to deliver a small surprise for just one of your team, or you decide to create an experience for every member of the organisation, from today, look for those moments, action those ideas. And create the magic!

In tune with your colleagues

Can you picture Kevin running frantically around the house in *Home Alone*? How about Elliott cycling in front of the full moon in *E.T.*? Could you divert your eyes away from the red coat in *Schindler's List*? Maybe you remember being as open mouthed as Dr Grant when you saw *Jurassic Park*? The opening amber scroll reaching far out to space from *Star Wars*? Or how about being petrified about swimming in the sea having seen *Jaws*?

We can all remember these iconic scenes and movies, but there is one crucial element that brings them all together. The element that heightens our sense, fusing the excitement and suspense to the imagery. That element is music. The score.

There is one person who binds this rich musical galaxy together. You won't see him, but you can always hear his work. Considered to be one of the greatest composers of our lifetime, he is John Towner Williams.

I am somewhat of a John Williams fan and, one way or another, I have his entire back catalogue, whether on CDs, vinyl or downloads. So when I received tickets for my birthday to see the Royal Philharmonic Orchestra perform 'The Music of John Williams', I knew I was in for a magical night. We sat mesmerised inside the Sunderland Empire Theatre, in awe of the music that simply took us back to a time when popcorn didn't require a second mortgage.

For me John Williams is Mr Star Wars. He composed the score of every film in the Skywalker saga since it began in 1977.

Despite playing a huge role in its phenomenal success, John never appeared on screen. That was until the very last movie – *The Rise of Skywalker*.

The director, JJ Abrams, and producer, Kathleen Kennedy, approached John and persuaded him to appear in just one scene. For a split second you can see him making his cameo appearance as Oma Tres (an anagram of Maestro), as a bartender on the planet Kajimi.

And this is when the production team chose to create a wonderful piece of Celebrity Service.

Abrams and the set designers decided for the brief moment John would appear on screen that he should be surrounded by nods to his illustrious career as a movie composer. The crew designed and built

51 different props to look like droid parts or junk, each of which was a tribute to one of John's previous 51 Academy Award nominations.

'We thought it would be fun to do something as a kind of celebration of what he has done and who he is,' Abrams said.

On the day of filming, the crew unveiled the set and the unique one-off props they had designed for John. These included the barricades from Omaha Beach in *Saving Private Ryan*, the iron from *Home Alone* and the spaceship from *E.T.*

Watching the 'making of' documentary, it was truly amazing to witness the detail and the lengths the entire team had gone to for just one person. John was already a star. He was already a celebrity. But it didn't stop the team from creating such a stunning personalised piece of Celebrity Service for one of its own.

What makes this more intriguing is this: you can pause it as much as you want but it's very difficult to see any of the props. You see they are not there for the fans, for the audience to like or share. They are there solely for one person.

Since the movie was released, John has received his 52nd Oscar nomination, for the movie he appeared in.

I'm now wondering... as you read this story, are you doing either (or both) of the following things...

1. Thinking of what you and your team could do for 'one of your own'?

2. Humming or whistling a tune or two? *Possibly Indiana Jones*? Maybe *Harry Potter*? How about *Superman*? Or *Close Encounters of The Third Kind*?

I'll leave it with you...

INTERVIEW

JAMES FOICE

CHIEF EXECUTIVE OF ASAP

ASSOCIATION OF SERVICED
APARTMENT PROVIDERS

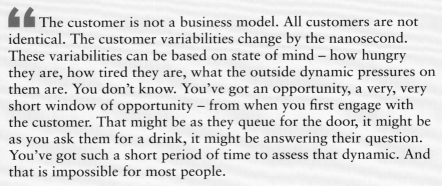

There's not many folk with as much experience and knowledge of providing a great customer experience as James. He has worked alongside Michelin chefs and Sir Richard Branson while at Virgin Atlantic and is currently setting the standards worldwide with ASAP.

" The customer is not a business model. All customers are not identical. The customer variabilities change by the nanosecond. These variabilities can be based on state of mind – how hungry they are, how tired they are, what the outside dynamic pressures on them are. You don't know. You've got an opportunity, a very, very short window of opportunity – from when you first engage with the customer. That might be as they queue for the door, it might be as you ask them for a drink, it might be answering their question. You've got such a short period of time to assess that dynamic. And that is impossible for most people.

It was only later on in life that I realised that if you don't get that bit right, the whole experience can change very quickly because you might misread someone. The biggest lesson I had was when I was working as a night porter in a hotel. I was a cocky little 18-year-old lad who thought he knew how to deal with people. And I misread a situation significantly. I'd served somebody some food in the restaurant and there was great banter throughout the evening – the customer seemed to be having really good fun with me. At the end of the night, as I cleared the table I asked, 'How was everything?' and he said, 'That was absolutely horrible.' Most waiters have heard this a million times. We've all enjoyed this sort of camaraderie with customers. Except I misread it. He was being serious. He pinned me up against the wall by my throat and I have never forgotten it. So that was my learning, about reading the customer and spotting the trigger points. In my world, it was a dining customer, but it could happen with any interaction, with a bank clerk or a staff member at the supermarket, it could be anyone. For anybody dealing with customers, you've got a very small window to assess the dynamic and get it right.

As you gain more experience with customers along with a recognition of what they need, then the parameters can be pushed. You can go beyond delivering what they want, surprising them. Doing something that the customer wasn't expecting and the impact that had on the whole hospitality experience was phenomenal and incredibly powerful. That very tiny element of surprising the customer, whoever they are, by just doing something different.

One of my colleagues at the hotel was a full-time night porter. Every Friday, this charming bloke would get his wages. He would take his pay packet, walk into Cheltenham, and buy a bouquet of flowers. And every Friday morning, without fail, he would give the flowers to the first woman that he saw.

He was even written about in the papers. I asked him, 'Why do you do this when you are happily married?' He said, 'That's not the point. What I'm doing here is recognising my day off.' He got to Friday every week, looking forward to his weekend and started his few days off by doing something special for somebody else. It was something he could control – to set the tone, his expectations and his whole mindset for the whole weekend.

If I've got a really good telephone call to make, say I want to praise somebody, or if there's an email I know is going to be really well received, I'll deliver it at the point that has the maximum impact for both parties. It's gonna make them feel good. It's going to make me feel good, too. So when do I want to do that? That's for me to control so that it has the maximum impact. It's about planning the timing of delivery of both the positives and negatives.

Last thing on a Friday is a really good time to drop the good news bomb, 'You have done an amazing thing this week. Thank you very much.' If this is the last thing they hear before they go off for their weekend it will have the maximum impact on their wellbeing, state of mind, motivation.

What is YOUR number one customer service superpower?

Not being frightened of getting things wrong.

It's OK. It's really OK to get things wrong. If you get it wrong, learn from it and know how to handle the situation. Don't lie about getting it wrong, tell somebody you've got it wrong and say, 'I'm so sorry we have made a mistake but this is how we're going to recover from the situation.'

What three things can any business or organisation do right now to create a greater Celebrity Service experience?

1. Talk to your customers, talk.

2. Think differently about how you communicate with your members or customers.

   Recently we wrote to all of our members. I mean we wrote a letter. It wasn't a handwritten letter, but it was hand-signed and we posted it. I couldn't believe the reaction on social media. Within a couple of days, pictures of the letter were taken and posted and scanned on to social media. There was just euphoria around a traditional method of communicating which is now no longer the norm.

3. Offer to help in times of turmoil. Or why not anytime really? Remind them that you are there.

What is the greatest customer service experience you've ever received?

I worked for Virgin for three years. Richard Branson is an interesting bloke, and quite an inspirational leader. He would open his doors once a year at his house in Kidlington and 20,000 staff and family would come over. He would put on a music festival with a bar, all quite wonderful. One year I took my oldest son, Christopher, who was quite young at the time.

We parked in the airfield, which was about two miles away and we were bussed onto the estate. There was an entrance towards the back of the estate, with a bridge over a brook. Richard Branson stood there for two hours, meeting and shaking hands with everybody coming into the park. Seeing my son's face when Richard Branson said, 'Welcome to my home. What's your name? Welcome. Nice haircut!' – that was very powerful. It's humanity, isn't it? Nobody is above that. You know, Christopher still talks about it now, 20 years on.

If you had a magic wand what would you wave it over to instantly ensure a greater service is delivered?

My magic wand would be putting all of the elements of business planning in place first rather than focusing on the bottom line and the profitability. That will come as long as you are able to manage costs and everything else. I'm not saying ignore it, but it's just getting it in the right order. Get your product right first.

What infuriates you most about customer service or the lack of?

Avoiding elements of true hospitality in order to focus on making the money.

PERSONALLY
SPEAKING

The questions you ask, the words you hear and the conversations you start can have an everlasting effect on the customer. Here are three of my favourites for you to enjoy.

We'll be back!

We landed at JFK airport and headed for the very first time to the Big Apple.

It was Hayley's 30th birthday and she had always wanted to see the Statue of Liberty. We took in so many of the tourist sites in the three days we were there, but there was one customer experience moment that particularly stands out.

It happened on the very first night. The big yellow cab dropped us off at the hotel. We flung our cases into the room and, not wanting to miss a minute of experiencing New York, we headed out into Times Square.

Our jet-lagged missions for the first evening were to take a photograph and to eat.

The photograph opportunity was to stand where my grandad once stood when he was stationed in New York during World War II. I didn't quite get to lean against the bar as he did, as the building's use had changed over the years, but technically I was there. Mission complete.

Gazing up at the bright lights and soaking up the sounds and the throng of the Times Square experience, it was time to attain our second goal. To eat.

At the entrance to Times Square there were two main restaurant brands adjacent to each other. On the left, Hard Rock Café and on the right, Planet Hollywood. We love the movies, so we turned right.

Hayley and I walked up the spiral staircase admiring the signed photographs of stars of the silver screen as we ascended. As we reached the top, a young lady behind a podium picked up two menus and said:

'Welcome to Planet Hollywood. Table for two is it?'

'Yes please.'

'Great, follow me.'

As we entered, I noticed a huge 8-foot Chewbacca costume on my right, and Hayley caught a glimpse of Sandy Dee's dress from Grease. We were in the movies.

'Are you guys here for business or pleasure?' she asked, weaving us through the busy restaurant.

'Pleasure,' I said.

'We came for a break as it's my birthday today,' Hayley replied.

'Oh, happy birthday! Would this table be okay for you?'

'Absolutely!' I said, enthusiastically.

Seated at our table for two, right behind Hayley's shoulder, inside a glass case, was a blood stained jacket riddled with bullet holes. I'll admit it wasn't the most romantic spot for a birthday meal but this was no ordinary jacket. It was Arnie's jacket from *The Terminator*!

We ordered drinks and starters.

In between our starters and mains the same waitress along with three of her colleagues hopped up on the leather seats beside us and sang *Happy Birthday* at the top of their voices. Everyone in the restaurant paused their conversations, looked over and joined in. Fun! Slightly embarrassing but mostly fun.

More drinks arrived and then dessert. And this is when it all happened.

The very same waitress who met us at the top of the stairs and who had sung her heart out, came across to collect our remaining dishes.

'Can I get you both anything else?'

Now this is the moment we'd normally ask for the bill. But we'd had so much fun and such a great experience that we decided to have one more round of drinks. I ordered a Budweiser and Hayley chose a cocktail from the menu. Minutes later the drinks arrived complete with sparklers and decoration. (At least, that's the cocktail, not my lager.)

There was more ice than alcohol left at the bottom of the cocktail glass, and I had just about finished my beer. The same waitress returned. This time she was stood beside me at an angle but her focus was very much on Hayley.

'Can I get you both anything else?'

'Just the bill please,' I said.

The waitress said 'Of course!' But then, looking straight at Hayley she said:

'Would you like to buy the glass?'

Hayley looked at me. I looked at Hayley and was secretly shaking my head, silently indicating we did not need to buy the glass.

And then the waitress added one of the finest customer experience lines ever.

'Would you like to buy the glass, as a souvenir, of your time here at Planet Hollywood on your *birthday?*'

Without hesitation Hayley said 'Oh yes!'

We knew with our shopping plans ahead of us on that trip, there would be no way we would fit this glass into what would be a bulging suitcase. On top of that, what was the price of the glass? We did not know.

Minutes later our waitress walked up to the table and handed Hayley a branded carrier bag. Inside was the actual glass used, now cleaned and polished and carefully placed inside a cardboard box surrounded by polystyrene.

From our conversation 90 minutes earlier, this waitress remembered why we were there. She panned for gold. She found the nugget. She spotted the opportunity and gave it back to us in a greater personalised experience.

To borrow and adapt the great Arnie's most iconic movie line... two nights later...

We were back.

Going bananas

Q. In a matter of seconds, how do you make your customers or potential customers feel great?

A. You compliment them.

You notice something you like about them, their family, their team or their business and you take the opportunity to tell them. But I wonder how often you or your colleagues really look to do this to make your customer feel wonderful in that moment, and indeed for the rest of their day?

Having already experienced many delights of the Big Apple including: Planet Hollywood (twice), the Empire State Building, the Rockefeller Centre, the Statue of Liberty – oh and not forgetting every floor of Bloomingdales and Macy's – we had reached the last day of our holiday and we had a few hours to kill before our flight.

So there we were, sitting outside Grand Central Station and we decided to complete our shopping exploits by venturing into the Banana Republic retail store.

Hayley turned left towards the ladieswear and I turned right. I picked up various items of clothing and entered the changing room, trying on a white t-shirt and a jumper. The full length mirror was just outside so I unlocked the door and pushed it open… just as a member of staff came bursting past with arms full of clothes piled up to her eyeballs. Bang! She hit the door. It swung wide and fast with my hand still attached to the handle.

Three paces later she stopped, swung round to point at me… and say…

'That sweater looks fab on you!'

She dashed off again to return her garment burden to shelves and rails. I never saw her again.

Meanwhile back in the changing area I was shocked and stunned. With my ego delightfully inflated I looked in the full length mirror. I was visibly two inches taller.

Now am I the only sucker for a compliment? Wouldn't you have felt great? Would you have gained two inches? Or perhaps you'd have that 'Ready Brek Glow' around you?

It took just a matter of seconds to make me feel great. I left the changing room and bought the t-shirt, the jumper and the same jumper in a different colour. (I do hope the shop assistant meant it.)

Compliments are one of the most underrated, underused and cost-effective ways to create a fantastic experience. Even with your hands full, rushing to get somewhere to get on with your busy life, you don't need to miss the opportunity. Just say something nice to someone today and watch that stardust land.

What's your daughter's name?

Since 2009 this story has appeared in just about every talk I have delivered. It is a great customer service engagement story and one of my all-time favourites.

Have you ever panned for gold? Maybe at a theme park or an outdoor activity centre, even back in the day when you were standing by a river in the Wild, Wild West? You'd take your metal pan and plunge it in the water. Seconds later you'd scoop up the sand and earth and lift it up into the shallow water where you'd give it a shake, allowing the excess water and sand to fall through the tiny holes in the pan. What you'd be looking for is a nugget, a golden nugget. A gem. A stone that could be worth a small fortune.

When it comes to engagement in the world of Celebrity Service it's all about finding that golden nugget. The panning for gold takes place during the conversations you have with the customer. The key is to listen out for the gemstone. To be alert for the piece of information that will help you to really engage. Once you've found it you can deliver a greater, more personalised experience.

This story is all about our daughter Grace. Two weeks before her fourth birthday, I was speaking at an event in the centre of London, which was due to finish around 2 pm but it actually finished a little earlier at 12 noon. I had a fixed ticket for the journey back and my train wasn't due to leave King's Cross station until 4 pm.

I now had four hours to spare in the capital. What would I do? How would I while away the hours until I was ready to jump on the train?

Let me tell you something about our Grace. She is very artistic. She loves to draw, paint, colour, stick and glue. We had already bought her the girl's bike and a particular doll she'd fallen in love with. She really didn't need anything else. However, right now here I am with time on my side. So I said to myself, I wonder if I could pick up a little art or craft gift in London? Something a little different? Something we couldn't buy back in the North East?

So I took a tube to Piccadilly Circus and proceeded to walk up Regent Street to a little toy store called Hamleys. You may know it. It is seven storeys tall and on the third floor is the girls' department.

The store layout is as follows: through the middle of the building there are the escalators that go all the way to the top and all the way to the bottom. On every one of the four corners on every level there is a table, which is used as a demonstration area. The Hamleys team take one of the toys, games or activities off

the shelf, unbox it and proceed to demonstrate it. And every time they do this, they create a piece of retail theatre that intrigues the shoppers and stops potential buyers in their tracks.

I reached the third floor and turned right. Immediately in front of me was a small table. On top of the table was an easel. On top of the easel was a large piece of white paper. In front of the table were a row of children all gathered around in a semicircle. Behind the children were the parents. Behind the parents was me... on my tip toes trying to take a peek at what the product was.

It was a grey plastic tray with six coloured slabs of paint and a brush. The demonstrator dipped the brush into the water and rolled the bristles over three colours at the same time. 'This, boys and girls, is how you do a butterfly...' She turned around and in a few strokes the girls and boys on the front row were open mouthed. She had just painted a multicoloured butterfly with one brush! Another dip into water, another roll across the paint slabs, this time when she turned she created a caterpillar. Everyone loved it.

'If you buy today you will receive a FREE stencil kit worth £10!' she pitched. The price of the grey plastic tray, six slabs of paint and a brush was £20. Half of the adoring crowd picked up the product to pop into their red Hamleys shopping bags. I was still standing there at the back, now wondering if I should buy this product for Grace. She'd love it. But she doesn't need it. But she'd love it.

And then it happened.

I had been spotted. Lady with the brush took four steps towards me. And asked the greatest, most engaging Celebrity Service question of all time…

'Is this for anyone special?'

Oh come on, what was I supposed to say to that? Her name badge said Julia.

'Yes…' And of course I spilled the beans.

'Yes, my daughter. She loves to cut, stick, glue and paint. It's her birthday in a couple of weeks' time and I am just looking for some ideas.'

'Ooh, if you buy today you'll receive a FREE stencil set worth £10!'

'Yes, I know, I've seen the whole show, but I've just walked in. In fact yours is the first thing I've seen and I don't know what else there is. So I am going to have a little walk around the shop, and if I don't see anything else, I'll pop back.'

And then came the second greatest, most engaging question of all time…

'What's your daughter's name?'

'Grace.'

Without missing a beat, Julia picked up the brush, dipped it into the water and rolled it over three colours. With a knowing glance towards me, she turned to the paper she'd used to create butterflies and caterpillars and all sorts and simply added the word GRACE.

She picked up the paper and turned slowly towards me, saying, 'If you don't find anything else you'd like, would you give this to Grace on her birthday from me.'

I handed over a £20 note.

Julia had found the golden nugget. She asked the question that would reveal the reason why I was interested in the product. She then found out the name of the person I wanted it for. Armed with this information she spotted the opportunity and took it.

This is why I have spoken about the brilliance of Julia and the wonderful Hamleys brand at every conference I've keynoted at around the world since 2009.

So I wonder who is talking about you? Which customer, client, guest, member or passenger has been singing your praises to everyone?

If we are not being talked about it's probably because we're not delivering an experience that deserves to be talked about.

* * *

I sat on the train at 15.55pm that afternoon, painting product stored overhead, as we pulled out of King's Cross station. One question kept coming back to me. What did Julia do to really connect with me? What did she do to make me want to hand over my money? There were two things. There was first a high degree of personalisation, and second there was full colour. She not only personalised her artwork with Grace's name but everything she did was bright and bold.

At Peterborough station I got out my laptop with these two reasons still fresh in my mind. I wondered, what can I learn from this? I opened up the proposal documents I was sending to prospective clients who had expressed an interest in me speaking at their next conference. Inspired by Julia I made numerous changes to the document, making them highly personal and injecting huge amounts of full colour.

The result? Since I changed the document that day on the train my bookings have increased by over 35 percent at proposal stage.

Here is my offer to you right now. If you are a business that sends out proposals and would like to see for yourself how and what I changed, simply email me **geoff@geofframm.com** and I will personally send the before and after documents to you.

INTERVIEW

MANDY SPENCER

COMMERCIAL DIRECTOR
ASPECTS HOLIDAYS

Mandy started working in the world of hospitality when she was 15 years old. She's been learning what 'great' looks like from an early age and continues to inspire her teams to this day.

" In customer service you can teach certain stuff. You can train people to behave in a certain way or to react in a certain way and be how you want them to be with the customer. But then there's people that just have it and you don't have to train them. Either way, we want to give customers a really great experience of booking with us; we do it because we want to do it, not because of what it might bring us in kudos. I think our ethic is just to be nice. It's as simple as that.

What is YOUR number one customer service superpower?

At Aspects we have an ability to connect to people. Whoever they are, we find common ground or some way of connecting with that person on a personal level. Not everybody wants to be connected with, I get that. Some people just want you to do your job and shut up. But for the most part, because it's holidays, it's not just placing an order, it's an experience. It should be fun and it should be exciting. A holiday is for all sorts of reasons, it could be just because it's a normal family holiday, it could be because it's been a terrible year, it could be because they're visiting someone. It's about finding out what that reason is and then making sure they understand that you know why it's so important. So I think if I wanted to put it in one word, it's probably empathy.

What is the greatest customer service experience you've ever received?

I'd been shopping in town and I'd tried on a few bits in the store. Later in the day I found I had an earring missing and knew I must have lost it in one of the shops. Normally, I'm not overly precious about material things but this was different as my son Jared had bought the earrings for me for my 40th birthday.

I rang all the shops I'd visited that day but no one was able to help. When I rang H&M it was different. The staff member was really helpful. Even though they were closing up, she said, 'I haven't found it, but I'm cleaning up now so I'll look for it.' I explained what it looked like. The next morning, I walked into the store and the girl popped up from behind the counter. She had not only found the earring, she had taken the trouble to wrap it up and she handed the small box back to me with a little note, 'How could I possibly not find something that was so precious that your son bought for you?' Oh, I was just blown away.

What three things can any business or organisation do right now to create a greater Celebrity Service experience?

1. Listen to your customers and get to know them.

2. Listen to your team and understand their strengths.

3. Come up with a new idea and run with it. And even if it doesn't work, do something else. Learn from it and don't give up.

What examples can you give me of how you or your team deliver a greater experience for your colleagues, teammates and employees?

In January when everyone's broke and fed up, we have a big housekeepers' party. There's normally 150 people there with a free bar, free food and they all just have a great night. The housekeepers aren't employed by us, but they are valued by us as they're people that we rely upon heavily and without them, we can't do what we do.

What infuriates you most about customer service or the lack of?

I hate the fact that people can be too efficient without being good!

There was this waitress, who was fast, very fast – actually too fast.

She was darting here, there and everywhere. But was there a smile? Was there any eye contact? Was there any desire to know who her customer was or interact with them? None. None at all. It was just a process of getting the job done. And for me, part of the whole process of eating out is that interaction and that kind of service element. Otherwise, I'd get a takeaway!

My daughter, Evie, wanted pasta, but she didn't want the kids' choice pasta. She wanted carbonara. I ordered a small portion of carbonara from the main menu. However, when it came to the dessert, Mum and I didn't really want anything but Evie wanted some ice cream and on the kids' menu was ice cream. I asked the waitress if Evie could just have a scoop of the vanilla and the chocolate ice cream? She said, 'No, sorry, that's on the children's menu and she didn't have the children's menu.' So we had a long discussion about this ice cream, I was offering lots of suggestions but the waitress was sticking to the fixed rules and couldn't seem to find a way to be flexible. She finally said, 'Oh, well, I'll have to ask the manager then.' And we did get the ice cream in the end, but it was hard work. Why would you stand there and think that was the right response? Why would you not just go, 'Oh, yeah, no problem, that's fine', and then go to your manager to explain? Why would you even have that discussion with the customer?

If you had a magic wand what would you wave it over to instantly ensure a greater service is delivered?

Give the people that work with you the opportunity to, or the empowerment to, make decisions. Don't insist on following the rule book to the letter. Give people the chance to do what they think is right for the customer.

If you had to place a customer service star along Hollywood Boulevard, whose name would be on it?

If I can name a profession, then teachers are the unsung heroes of customer service. They have to get to know 30 kids every year. They have to find out all about them, discover each of their foibles, their ins and outs, their little idiosyncrasies, all of those things… Evie's teacher, Mrs Peck, she's definitely up there because she's lovely and Evie loves her to bits.

When I was 15 I worked as a seasonal waitress/chambermaid at a small hotel in Carbis Bay. The owner was Marie Monk. She was more than a customer service star, she was my friend and became like a mentor to me. She dressed well and looked great. She chatted to everybody. She went round all the tables every night to talk to all of our guests. With her attention to detail throughout the hotel, she made sure it was just the best experience for the guests that it could be.

Marie wanted every guest to feel special and by treating her staff with the same care, she showed me how to get the best out of people, and give customers a genuinely great experience. She was my first mentor and Jennie Smith, Aspects founder, was my last. Both were incredible women that taught me so much.

CIARÁN PURCELL

HEAD OF RETAIL EXPERIENCE

PETER MARK

Ciarán's passion for hair emerged at three years old, while cutting the hair on his sister's Barbie dolls. Starting with Peter Mark at just 16 years of age his enthusiasm and passion for delivering a greater caring service has seen him rise through the ranks.

" There was a point in time when I felt we just weren't really talking to our clients about their hair or hair goals. So I started doing just that and from there I started creating hair plans for them, advising them to use a certain range at home for six weeks before coming back in for a hair re-assessment. One day, my former manager, Cathal, came down to me and told me there was a woman at the front desk who wanted to talk to me.

I wondered if I'd messed up someone's hair! I went to see and the woman introduced herself: 'My name is Valerie. You looked after my sister's hair last week. You recommended products for her and her hair feels amazing. What do you think of my hair? What should I use on my hair to get it the way I want it to be?' So I thought to myself, I've never met you before. You have driven to a shopping centre that's really difficult to park at. You've walked all the way to the top floor. You have come to a reception desk to ask to speak to someone you don't even know, to ask what you should be using for your hair.

So finding this new client really inspired me to make sure that every single person I met would get this level of service and advice.

Within three months I was in the top three requested stylists in the salon. And I was no 1 salesperson in the whole company.

What is the greatest piece of service you've seen at Peter Mark?

This particular client had just had her hair done and gone home. It was something like half six that evening, the salon was cashing up and the phone was ringing. The name of the client came up on the phone system display, so we knew who it was. When our receptionist answered the call, she couldn't really hear anything much, just a mumble. She knew it wasn't right, wasn't normal. So she hung up the phone and rang an ambulance giving them the customer's details. She'd actually had a stroke and we were the last number on her phone that she had called. At our management conference that year, our CEO, Peter, and the salon manager Laura, got that receptionist up on stage and gave her flowers. What she did for that client was above and beyond customer service. She saved her life.

What is YOUR number one customer service superpower?

It's quite simple really. I care about people. I genuinely care if they are happy or not.

What is the greatest customer service experience you've ever received?

I got married last October but ten days beforehand we realised we didn't have any rings. We went to two or three shops, and the fourth shop was StoneChat Jewellers. When we explained that there were just ten days until our wedding, the shop assistant was really excited, asking us lots of questions. She just seemed genuinely interested, which was lovely. Her name was Sophie.

She explained, 'What I'm gonna do is I'm going to check out every single ring colour that we have with your skin tone so we can see what actually looks best on you.' We spent quite some time trying on different rings, the one we chose in the end was 250 euros. I'd have gladly paid more but with Sophie's help this seemed to be the perfect ring. She didn't care about trying to sell us the most expensive ring. She wanted to make sure that what we had was actually the right one for us.

Of course, I've recommended four or five people now to go there because the experience was so good. That's what it's all about.

What three things can any business or organisation do right now to create a greater Celebrity Service experience?

1. You need to have a personality and show who you are. Be authentic in who you are.

2. Listen to what your clients want and be open to their feedback and act on it.

3. Be creative, up your game. Innovation is so huge and it's so, so important. Listen to what the client wants, but actually surprise them more. Go further than what the client has asked for.

If you had to place a customer service star along Hollywood Boulevard, whose name would be on it?

My manager at the Dundrum salon, Cathal Keaveney who I've worked with for 10 years. I've never met someone so client-focused in my whole life. He also has the most incredible positive energy that's clear from his body language. Even if the client was in the wrong, he would still say to them, 'We're so sorry that this is how you feel. What we're gonna do is…' And he would give them a complimentary gift. He inspires me still by always putting the client first and being the most positive person. So Cathal would be my Hollywood star.

CREATIVE
SPACES,
HAPPY FACES

JABBA THE CUTT BARBERS

📞 07825279563

PRICE LIST

WET CUT	£8.50
KIDS CUT	£7.00
OAP	£6.00
BEARD TRIM	£4.00
CREW CUT	£5.00
BLENDED CREW	£6.00
LONG HAIR	£9.00
VADER AND LUKE SPECIAL	£15.00

queue buster special...

bookings (via fb messenger or text) run between 5 & 6.30 on a friday
for . . . just add £2.50 to the price (£2.50 if mrs hair and beard) on
va . . .

. . . cutt.com

Have you ever entered a building and whispered under your breath 'Ooooh I wish I worked here'. What could you add to your workplace to put smiles on the faces of your team members and your clients? Here are some ideas...

Jabba the Cutt

So there we were on a two-week holiday in Cornwall. We checked the weather forecast for the next day and didn't fancy a trip to the beach in storm force winds and torrential rain. Instead we opted for a trip to the city of Truro. Grace and Elliot had some holiday money to spend, so off we went.

Devouring Cornish ice cream and the legendary pasties could have been the highlight of a very cold day until we found ourselves walking towards a rather interesting and exciting A-board.

It stopped me in my tracks. I had the biggest beam across my face.

I turned to Elliot, 'Would you like your hair cut?'

He looked somewhat puzzled, and then he saw the board... 'YES!!!!'

Elliot didn't really need his hair cutting and neither did I, but that wasn't going to stop us.

We said our goodbyes to Hayley and Grace who wandered off to another store. Elliot and I headed up a cobbled street to where the A-board sign was pulling us in.

We arrived at Jabba the Cutt. I kid you not, we had found a *Star Wars* themed barber shop! The brand was bright and bold from the outside, but we had no idea what to expect once inside.

The owner was a gentleman called Mark Richards who had turned his boyhood love and passion into a very successful business.

As soon as we got inside, our eyes were treated to a galaxy of memorabilia. There were books, games, magazines, posters, pictures, figurines, video games... it was like walking into the childhood bedroom you'd always dreamt of. Only without the smell of hair gel. Beyond the actual stuff, there was another reason that Jabba the Cutt strongly featured both Jedi and Sith. Yes the team were great barbers, but they also had great conversation.

'Who is your favourite character?' Mark asked Elliot. And 'What's your best movie?' Not 'What school do you go to?' or 'Going anywhere nice this weekend?'. Elliot was in his element and he loved every minute of being in the Emperor's Chair. (How many children can say that I wonder?)

Mark said, 'As a huge *Star Wars* fan (as well as a master barber) I wanted to create a space that I would enjoy working in and a place that customers would also find fun and quirky. And so, Jabba the Cutt was born and it's been going from strength to strength ever since.'

Jabba the Cutt has character. It delivers an experience. An experience we will never forget.

Yet out of the whole experience, the bit that resonated most with me was Mark's comment, 'I wanted to create a space that I would enjoy working in'. I wonder, as you read that line, if you might be asking yourself: do you have a workplace environment that you enjoy working in? Maybe you don't right now, but how might you change it so you do?

There was just one very big downside to our adventure. I had to inform Elliot we would have an 898-mile return drive for any future appointments.

The search to find a vehicle to help us jump to lightspeed is well underway.

Sith happens

If I had to stay in just one place for the rest of my life I'd probably choose 351 Studio Drive, Lake Buena Vista, 32830 – also known as… Hollywood Studios, Disney World, Florida. It's a theme park that as a family we love more than any other. It was a long time ago that we first went there. Elliot was 3, Grace was 9. Inside the theme park you will find the Star Wars Launch Bay. It's practically a whole museum of memorabilia with posters, outfits, vehicles, props. You name it, it's in there. There are also two meet-and-greet experiences. No Mickey, Donald or Minnie this time. If you turn left you will meet Chewbacca. If you turn right it's Kylo Ren.

For the first meet-and-greet we chose the light side and stood in the 45-minute queue to meet the 8-foot Wookiee. As we neared the door the anticipation mounted – we could hear the muffled roars, but couldn't see a thing. Catching my first glimpse I froze momentarily. It was as if I was looking skywards at the late Peter Mayhew himself.

If you go, you'll find he's very well behaved. He will hug you, ruffle your hair, and stand really still while your family photos are taken. He even said goodbye to Hayley in his own Wookiee voice as we left the room laughing.

It was such a wonderful experience, with all the parts played superbly in character.

Five days later we returned to this, our favourite of all the parks – this time to take the rides and experience the attractions we had missed the first time. Toy Story Mania! followed Rope Drop and then there was just one more character to meet. The Supreme Leader of the First Order, Kylo Ren.

We entered the Launch Bay and turned right. Around 40 minutes later (he wasn't quite as popular as Chewie) we were ready to enter the room.

And then everything changed.

Cloaked in black, mask in place, the son of Han Solo and Leia Organa menacingly strode up to us all. Elliot clung on to Hayley and spontaneously burst into tears. Grace grabbed my hand and also burst into tears. Meanwhile Hayley and I burst out laughing. (Does this make us bad parents?)

The children were so shocked, alarmed and frightened by this entire episode that they no longer wanted their photograph taken. They stood at the back of the room clinging to their mother while I stepped forward to have the photograph taken. Kylo was communicating through the mask in his onscreen voice. It was all very surreal. Yet it was also very real and quite an authentic experience.

A few more pics were taken and thankfully I could see both Elliot and Grace had calmed down after their initial traumatic contact with the new villain of the galaxy.

The shoot ended and as I collected the scanned notification on my wrist band, Kylo Ren strode up once again to Elliot, inches away, face to face, and said, 'I WILL FIND YOU!'

Thanks mate, thanks a lot. It took Elliot a further two hours to calm down and a further three nights of controlled, supportive bedtime routines to convince him Kylo Ren wasn't going to come and get him while he was on his holiday in Florida.

I have to say, I thought long and hard whether this was an experience worth sharing in this book. The reason it made the cut was because of, beyond anything else, its authenticity. It was terrifying, yes, and probably not really appropriate and yet it was done brilliantly and 'for real'.

You can't fake Celebrity Service; you can't just switch from the light to the dark and then back again. Remain authentic, remain consistent, or people will see through your mask.

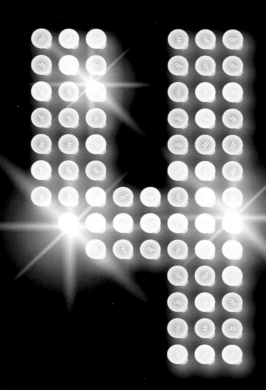

THE 120
CHALLENGE

Over the moon, proud, delighted and amazed, just some of the words I'd describe the effects that generate from the 120 Challenges.

This is a technique I created a long time ago. I was looking to introduce a quick-fire, highly interactive section within my talks that would bring about maximum engagement with any team or audience.

They needed to be short in length so 2 minutes would be perfect. 120 seconds would certainly be challenging for everyone to focus on the issue, solve a problem or improve any touchpoint in a very short passage of time.

They did just that, but what I hadn't quite anticipated were the results of this 120 creation. When I say results I mean ideas. Amazing thoughtful ideas and cost-effective suggestions, teams and organisations simply never had before.

Throughout the world and with every sector imaginable the 120 Challenge has never failed to generate ideas and experiences teams could then use the very next day.

In short it's a quick-fire round of pure creativity, ideas and inspiration. But the longer term impact is a technique you can easily adopt to maintain and improve Celebrity Service momentum in your business or organisation.

Take any customer touchpoint, process or piece of communication and give it a 120 make-over and you will realise this most simplest of techniques will breathe fresh, creative ideas into your business.

What you need

How many can play?
You need to work in teams; you can do this as a duet or with up to eight people per team depending on the size of your department or business.

How many teams?
There needs to be a level of competition so try and create three teams; I have also done this with over 50 teams. Warning! The more teams the louder it will become so bring your earplugs.

Equipment

Plain paper and coloured felt tip pens, a stopwatch or egg timer. Flipcharts if you have them or just use a table to rest on.

How to play

Give your teams the exact same challenge, maybe something that inspired you recently. Describe the story to the teams and without revealing the amazing piece of service or experience ask them in 120 seconds what they would have done to improve the experience and service?

Timing

Start the clock. Halfway through give your teams a 1-minute warning, 30-seconds warning and then loudly count down 5,4,3,2,1… stop! Put down your pens. Who wants to share their ideas with the room first?

Results

Let every team reveal their ideas. Let everyone contribute to the challenge. Now record all of these ideas by either taking a photograph of the papers or writing down the best ones on the board. Prizes can now be given out to the winners of most creative, most cost-effective, most crazy, etc.

Prizes

Give your team an incentive (sweets, Celebrity Service 120 Trophy, drinks vouchers, day off work, basically anything to reward and recognise their great creative answers).

Observational tip

When one team reveals their answers, carefully listen to the reaction in the room. If you hear gasps, giggles or a round of applause, something clearly resonated with your team, and you might want to take this idea and develop it further.

Once the 120 Challenge has concluded you can now reveal the ideas you experienced from the question you set. You see the 120 Challenge isn't a fictitious question to spark everyone's imagination, it is a real-life scenario, and this is what your teams will be inspired by the most. Real people in real situations delivering real-life service excellence.

So you now know its origins and how you introduce this to your business or organisation, but let me set the ball rolling for you now with the first 120 Challenge of Celebrity Service Superstars…

Waving a magic wand over your business

If there is one thing I love it's creativity. I just love those people and businesses who spot an opportunity and create a magical piece of communication that leads to a memorable experience.

Despite living only a couple of hours away, we'd never attended the Edinburgh Fringe comedy festival. When my good friend Jeremy Nicholas announced he was performing his month-long, one-man show, we just had to go to see him. Arriving in the Scottish capital, the streets were full to the brim with comedy seekers searching for their next chuckle.

On the way to the venue we noticed a rather large crowd standing outside a café. Could some comedy performer be trying out new material ad hoc, or maybe someone famous was signing autographs? Or maybe it was the café itself? They must have the greatest coffee or perhaps amazing homemade cakes and scones? Or, with my marketing hat on, could there be a great offer to tempt us?
Or perhaps they were handing out free samples?

A crowd will always attract a crowd, so we walked over and I moved in closer to see what was drawing these customers in. I noticed many of the people queuing were taking photographs of the café window, in particular a sun-faded sign.

Wow! So this is a place J K Rowling, one of the world's most famous writers, used to frequent. From inside these four walls of The Elephant House café she would write what would become the global phenomenon, *Harry Potter*. Of course, every true fan knows about this place and they all want to visit. I guess they want to feel a connection and to see where it all began.

Imagine if you will that you were the owner of The Elephant House? You'd think all of your birthdays had come at once. What a wonderful unique selling point you have. A great café, fantastic food and drink, and now a global tourist destination magnet to match. Magic.

Now let's look at this standing in someone else's shoes. Imagine you were a potential competitor? Imagine you were nearby and offered similar products, drinks, food, and so on? You'd be highly disadvantaged, right?

Not necessarily.

120 Challenge

Here is your first 120 Challenge. You have 2 minutes (120 seconds) to create a stunning piece of Celebrity Service magic of your own.

You are the competitor in question. You have a café right across the road from The Elephant House. You also have a window, but what sign would you put in there?

Whatever you write, remember the goal is to heighten the experience for your own customers.

Turn to THE BIG REVEALS on page 157.

INTERVIEW

SUMILA: DYNAMIC DUO

SUSANNE CLARKE
HEAD OF SERVICE EXCELLENCE

DR CAMILA DEVIS-ROZENTAL
SENIOR ACADEMIC, SERVICE EXCELLENCE AT BOURNEMOUTH UNIVERSITY

What is the greatest piece of service you've seen at Bournemouth University?

One of our bus drivers, Robbie, does a two-mile trip across the two campus buildings for our students who need to get from one building to another. That's what he does. Yet, every year the students nominate him for so many 'You're Brilliant' awards. He was even the gold winner one year and was given the opportunity to go to the Queen's Garden Party. He's not even technically an employee of ours; he's a partner. Because he loves his job so much, he just cheers everyone up the moment they walk on his bus.

I know, because if I get on his bus I feel like a princess, like the most important person he's seen all day. And all he ever really says is 'Hello, are you alright?' but you can just feel that energy of his on the bus. The students get on the bus about 40 percent awake, seeing his beaming smile they just wake up. It's a lovely example of somebody who loves what he does and puts every part of his personality into it.

What is YOUR number one customer service superpower?

Camila

Susanne's superpower is that she has an ability to take a 'helicopter view' of a situation. This means that she can very, very quickly pick up what is needed and then go on to make it happen. Perception and passion form part of that.

Susanne

Camila's superpower is positivity – seeing that there is always a way to resolve things.

What is the greatest customer service experience you've ever received?

We were holidaying in Disney and had booked a disabled room in advance at one of the 2-star rated hotels. When we got there the room we had been given wasn't accessible. There had also been a few other issues so my husband went to reception to complain. 'Let's just see what we can do,' they said before coming back to Joe with a solution. They'd found somewhere else for us to stay with proper disabled amenities.

They took us in a little cart to a 5-star hotel. We stayed for the five days that we had paid for a 2-star hotel in a 5-star hotel! I'll never forget, when we opened the door to the new room, my children and I started laughing nervously. It was hard to believe but this place it was bigger than our house! And we never paid an extra penny. They were just so apologetic about it. So whenever I try to solve things with people, I always want them to feel like that.

What three things can any business or organisation do right now to create a greater Celebrity Service experience?

Susanne

1. Service excellence and understanding how to develop that service heart and mindset in a team.

2. Having the right offer, the right product, the right service.

3. The right delivery mechanisms to make it easy for customers.

Camila

The three Ps

1. Purpose – knowing what you are doing and why you are doing it.

2. Passion – making sure you have the right people on board who love what they do.

3. Privilege – everyone realising how lucky they are that they get to do what they do, regardless of what they do.

What examples can you share of how you or your team deliver a greater internal experience?

Susanne

We give everybody a voice. It doesn't matter to us whether they're senior managers or junior people. So we'll make time in our diary for everyone. We want everyone to feel important and appreciated.

Camila

I think the way we communicate with people in our emails is very personal. We always make a point to remember who they are and what their particular needs are.

What infuriates you most about customer service or the lack of?

Camila

I hate rude emails. I hate them so much! When you send a really nice email and then someone just replies with 'Cheers' or not even that.

Susanne

It's lack of responsibility and not owning the problem that infuriates me. That's one thing that's really important to us that we've got right across the whole institution – that we all take some form of ownership.

If you had a magic wand what would you wave it over to instantly ensure a greater service is delivered?

Susanne

I think it's kindness. I think if we were just all kinder to each other the service we give would improve.

Camila

I think it would be empathy. Treat others as you would like to be treated. Don't assume things of other people before you know them. I think that's a really important thing. I think if we are able to put ourselves in someone else's shoes, we may not feel the same as they do, but we may be able to try to acknowledge how important something is to them. If we did that with everyone, we'd deliver service excellence because we'd be really getting into what's important to that person.

If you had to place a customer service star along Hollywood Boulevard, whose name would be on it?

Susanne
Camila, she just exudes positivity and she's got this magic ingredient that just lifts everyone she comes into contact with.

Camila
Susanne, she lives by what she believes, she is the example of service excellence for me.

PROBLEM,
WHAT
PROBLEM?

Things will always break. Things will always fail to arrive. It's life. But be ready to turn any negative situation into a positive experience with the following ideas...

Lost and hound

It's easy to think a great customer experience is all about the person directly in front of you – the person holding the purse, wallet, contactless card or signed contract. In fact, true Celebrity Service looks beyond the customer and focuses on the customer's loved ones too.

Let's visit Aspects Holidays once again...

The team at Aspects don't only provide an amazing experience for their holidaying customers. They do that for their four-legged visitors too.

As families arrive at their holiday properties their dog will also receive its very own welcome pack. A guide for their stay includes a list of dog friendly places to eat as well as the best beaches for their pet to play on and waters to plodge in.

Best of all... inside the welcome pack is a dog tag which is provided by Aspects Holidays. With the easily recognisable tag around the dog's neck, should the dog ever lose its way in an unfamiliar place, the dog can be brought safely back to one of their local offices.

At the time of writing, there has yet to be a dog who became lost, and then found, and then returned to the offices. So is there any real need to go to the trouble of investing the time and money to supply the tags? Only Celebrity Service Superstars would think like this. Their 'just in case' strategy may one day be the greatest thing to have ever happened to one of their visitors. We never know what's around the corner but where the loss of a dog on its holidays is concerned, Aspects have it covered.

Sliding Doors on an aircraft

I love Australia.

The sight of the Sydney Harbour Bridge and the Opera House are truly breathtaking. As for Melbourne, well, I could easily live there. Perth, Brisbane, the Gold Coast, all of it. I just love it.

However, travelling there is another story. It's not the shortest of journeys I'll ever make. But it's a lot less daunting when you break it down into three 7-hour flights. That's all it is.

Newcastle International Airport is only a 30-minute drive from our home and at 1 pm daily Emirates take to the skies to Dubai. From Dubai it's another 7-hour flight to Kuala Lumpur. Then there is a 90-minute stopover to disembark and stretch your legs, while they prepare the aircraft and change crew. The final 7-hour leg is Kuala Lumpur to your Australian city of choice.

Thankfully you have the movies. Copious amounts of movies. As well as documentaries of course. And music. All on tap to help while away the hours. Imagine if there were no entertainment on board!!!

Let me take you back to one of my journeys down-under; in this instance I was on the first leg, Newcastle to Dubai. The staff were great, the food was wonderful and everyone settled down to enjoy the latest blockbuster. Seats were reclined, remote controls in hand… and it's off we go…

There was just one slight problem. Of all the screens on board, mine was the only one not working. It was totally blank. I called the team, who rebooted the system (a nifty inflight version of Ctl Alt Delete). The screen came alive. Shortly afterwards, blank again. Rebooted again. And again. Alas it was not meant to be. They apologised profusely and I said no problem at all, these things happen – this gives me a chance to read my book.

Many years ago Hayley and I saw *Sliding Doors* at the cinema and it's been one of our favourite movies ever since. We are great believers in those *Sliding Doors* moments in life.

I turned the overhead spotlight on to illuminate my first page and began to read. I had just completed the opening chapter when I heard giggling. A few more minutes passed and the giggling returned. This wasn't the staff sharing a joke. I heard the distinctive sound of children. Young children. Halfway through chapter two and the volume of giggling increased. By this stage everyone around me was either watching their screens or had fallen asleep, so I seemed to be the only one listening to the sound of hilarity.

The intrigue finally got to me. I placed my book in the pocket, unbuckled the seatbelt, removed the blanket and stood up. I drew back the curtain.

There sitting on the floor were two little girls, probably around 4 and 6 years old. And on the floor with them were three members of the Emirates cabin crew (I won't guess their age). I couldn't see the floor for colouring pens, colouring books and board games.

A fourth member of the crew, Tarik, standing beside them in the galley apologised for disturbing me. I said it wasn't a problem, it was rare and a treat to hear children laughing at 36,000 feet. He offered me one of his 'speciality' coffees to which I said yes. (Let's just say it had a kick to it.)

Tarik was also taking photographs on a polaroid camera. Within a minute of being taken, the picture would slowly reveal itself and the team would slide it into a branded photo sleeve for the girls to take with them as a souvenir of their flight.

I stood chatting with the team for about half an hour and it was then that I found out what they had really done.

Further down the aircraft a mum travelling alone with her three young children was desperately trying to settle her baby girl to sleep. The crew said she had tried for a long time without success. The mum was also trying to entertain her other two daughters who were wide awake. The Emirates team spotted this and offered to take the two girls up to the galley to play with them to give Mum more space and time with her baby. Dimi, Paige and Courtney took the girls to the galley, gathering up plenty of activities for their entertainment.

A few 'speciality' coffees later and the team were now taking photographs of me. Before I left the plane they gave me my own souvenir images together with a handwritten note.

Gwyneth Paltrow missed the train one day and her life changed forever. That night I missed a movie, but in true *Sliding Doors* fashion that led to me sharing this story of something I might never have witnessed – a Celebrity Service Superstar team spotting an opportunity to change the experience of a family and make a massive difference in that moment.

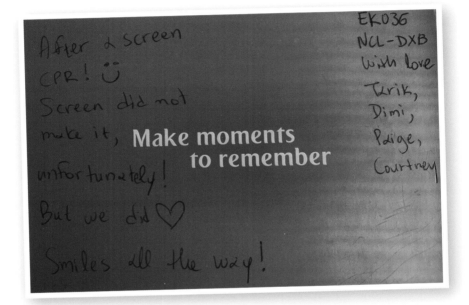

Touchpoint, touchdown Cowboys

This one would turn out to be a trip I will never forget.

It had been 18 months earlier that I'd received a message asking if I would speak on the main stage at the National Speakers Association (NSA) main convention in Dallas, Texas.

Now, this might need to be put into some context...

The NSA Convention is a convention for speakers. You read that right. It's a convention of speakers speaking to speakers! It is a fabulously inspiring four-day meeting and, boy oh boy... everyone loves to talk! To be honest I wouldn't be surprised to find that when each speaker returns to their hotel bedroom, as soon as they open the mini bar and the light comes on, they do a quick 10-minute talk.

Each year, over 2000 professional speakers from all over the world converge into one venue to learn, share, develop their craft and meet old and new friends.

It was a huge honour to have been asked. I later found out I was the only Englishman ever to have been invited to keynote on their main platform. I couldn't resist. I said yes.

The conference was truly amazing. I admit it's probably the most nervous I've ever felt, waiting in the wings as my intro was read out and the walk on music started. My 20 minutes went past in a flash. A wonderful standing ovation followed and now I could relax.

And to relax there was only one place to go... the AT&T Stadium, the home of the Dallas Cowboys. The farewell party on the last day of the NSA conference was to be held at the stadium, but earlier that same day my speaker buddy Dean Lindsay and I took the full stadium tour. We had already visited the grassy knoll earlier in the day and now it was time to visit the $1.15 billion dollar, 80,000 capacity arena.

I love stadium tours. It's not just the sporting side, it's also the business behind the game that intrigues me. I learned that their indoor giant screen is one of the largest high-definition screens in the world. Turn it on its axis and it's as tall as a seven-storey building. They can also increase the capacity for a Super Bowl or when U2 come to town by removing all of the armrests and pushing the seats together to add more seats to each row. Genius.

The tour guide also told us that they had more drink and food concessions than any other team in the US. When a member of the tour party asked why, she said 'We don't want you to stand in line, wasting time when you could be giving us money...'. Clever.

One of the endzones was sponsored by automotive giant Ford, but when you looked more closely you could see they had built an elevated showroom with space for six vehicles. Unbelievable.

As the tour was coming to an end we were given a choice by the guide. We could either go pitch-side or go to the store for the remaining time we had left. Dean went pitch-side while I opted to go and purchase some souvenirs for the office. I picked up some pens and pencils for Grace and Elliot and a miniature Dallas Cowboys helmet. (Whenever I speak in the US I purchase a team helmet of the city I'm visiting.) Standing in the queue, I was next to be served but as I placed the items on the counter the chip and pin card system powered down. They could no longer take debit or credit cards. 'No problem,' said the staff member, 'We can still take cash.' Ah, I didn't have a cent on me. Problem? You'd think so. Not for the Cowboys!

'Would you like to take a secret tour?' the cashier whispered over the counter.

Who wouldn't? Where would I go? What would I see? A special experience was about to begin.

Another member of staff walked over to help me. She escorted me through the store, into the stock room, down the stairs, along the concourse, up some more stairs and to the cash point machine back inside the stadium. There I withdrew the dollars needed and we headed back. (It was a secret tour that Dean and the others hadn't seen.)

As we approached the till my gifts were already waiting in a bag for me and as my escort departed she said, 'For your troubles we have deducted 20 percent off your bill.' Result. Extra point.

After one technical glitch they took ownership of the problem, and then turned it into a great piece of Celebrity Service experience.

The stars that adorn the Dallas helmet is just an image, but I found real Superstars that day working inside the greatest stadium I'd ever seen.

When things go wrong (and inevitably they will), how can you turn it around? What can you say? And what twist at the end can you deliver to make it an experience your customer will never ever forget?

INTERVIEW

SARA DAVIES

FOUNDER & CREATIVE DIRECTOR

CRAFTER'S COMPANION

Sara Davies of Crafter's Companion was one of my very first clients. Even if you're not an avid crafter, you may know her as a dragon investor on the BBC show Dragons' Den.

" The biggest driver for me to set up business was because I love customers. I fell totally in love with the customers in this crafting space. People who do advanced crafts generally don't just do it as a hobby. It's so much more. It's a passion. It's a way of life. A lot of them are older retired people. They may be widowed or have had health issues and have taken up craft as a way to get through. A lot of people take up crafts for the wellbeing benefits. And so for them, it's a lifeline and they are so passionate about it. I really wanted to start a business in this industry because the customer base is colossal. And so I did. I had a head full of magic, a load of ideas. I was going back off to university for the final year but I couldn't even wait until I graduated. I needed to get a start with this business in case somebody else had the same ideas that I'd had.

What is the greatest piece of service you've seen at Crafter's Companion?

We invest really heavily in social media, but not just by putting out Instagram stories and Facebook posts. We create communities. Our typical customer, especially on Facebook, is usually an older lady who likes to be part of a community. If we were to put something on the Crafter's Companion wall, they might look at it, but it's corporate it's not personal. So we've created these groups, these communities that our customers can be a part of.

A great example is the shopping channel that we work with, HSN. We created a fan group called Fans of Crafter's Companion on HSN. And we have a little army of professional level crafters – there are about 30 of them who are on what you might call our design team. Every month we send them a box-load of products and they make samples to send us that we use in our YouTube clips. And they go onto the HSN TV channel. These crafters receive a design team badge and they get to put on their Facebook page that they work as a Crafter's Companion design team member. They are in the fold. They get staff discount on all of our products as well. So we make them feel really special. But part of their role is to engage with our customers on our behalf. A lot of people wouldn't have the confidence even on their own page on Facebook to show a picture of what they'd made. But they would go into a group where there are other like-minded crafters and show it there.

What is YOUR number one customer service superpower?

I can be very persuasive and I think it's because I'm always very positive about everything. Someone even said to me the other day, 'You are the only person I know who can make a no sound like a yes.' If I'm in one of our stores and there's a customer complaining, I can go over to them and engage in conversation with them but because I just pour a ridiculous amount of honey on it and I'm just so nice about everything, they can't help but be nice back.

What three things can any business or organisation do right now to create a greater Celebrity Service experience?

1. Definitely exceed expectations.
2. Create raving fans.
3. Surprise, surprise and delight.

What examples can you share of how you or your team deliver a greater internal experience?

One of the staff implemented something about a year ago, which was little cards. So if someone in the business has done something really nice for you, you write a message on a little card and it gets stuck on a pin board. I thought that was lovely!

If you had a magic wand what would you wave it over to instantly ensure a greater service is delivered?

The most important thing in our stores is that the customers are inspired to do more crafts. What I want is for someone to walk through the door in one of my stores and for a staff member just to be able to sit down with them, talk about what sort of crafts they are into, ask questions, genuinely engage and just spend more time with the crafting customers. So that's one thing I would love to change with the wand, to allow more time for the in-store staff to talk to the customers.

If you had to place a customer service star along Hollywood Boulevard, whose name would be on it?

Kids First nursery where my kids both went had a supervisor called Megan Goodman. When my eldest, Oliver, started he was nine months old and she was the key worker there. As a parent you obviously feel really nervous about it, but I felt like she looked after him so well. I was devastated when he moved into the next class because she wasn't going to be there as she was staying with the younger class. And even though it's not her job to do this, she still used to go every day to check on Oliver. At the end of the day when I would pick him up, she'd come through and say, 'I know you were worried so I've had a chat with the team in Oliver's room.' She did that all the way through nursery for Oliver. She was one of 40 staff there, in one room out of eight rooms. Oliver moved through each room as he got older and she made a point of checking in every day. As a mother, the way my kids were cared for was so important and so when Charlie started I insisted that Megan was going to look after him too. She now babysits for Oliver and Charlie at home. She is exceptional.

WHAT A WONDERFUL WORLD

When your back's against the wall you can freeze, do nothing or come back stronger. You can reveal your creativity and your resilience. Just like the following people and their businesses.

A year that changed everything

Ah, the year 2020. A new decade. A year full of hope. A year brimming with new ideas and adventures. A year… oh hang on, let's start again…

Ah, the year 2020. The year the world changed. The year our grandchildren and our great grandchildren will forever study at school along with the dinosaurs, the Roman Empire, World War II and the sinking of the *Titanic*.

A year where the best thing most of us could do to help, was to do nothing.

A year when we heard the word furlough for the first time and our window panes glowed with a rainbow of hope.

A year that would bring out the very best in people. And the very best in businesses too. Of course there were those brands who didn't quite reach the Dunkirk spirit level, but this isn't the place for them and this certainly isn't the book to dwell on negativity. (It's hard to be inspired by negativity.)

A year in which decisions were made about how we really looked after our teams and customers. A time when those subtle things called ethics, character and heart were wonderfully exposed for the world to see.

So, what exactly did we see?

In truth there could be an entire book devoted to those who did the right thing during the Covid-19 crisis. But I wanted to highlight my own personal collection of those who selflessly saw an opportunity to do the right thing, the creative thing and then made it happen.

I give you the Superstars of 2020…

Love coffee

Pret A Manger were one of the first to react. Their posting across social media simply said: 'Dear NHS Workers, your hot drinks are now on the house from today and we'll take 50% off everything else. Thank you for everything you are doing. We look forward to serving you. With love, everyone at Pret.'

Hair today, given away tomorrow

The Wella Professional hair brand also gave away their wonderful products with the message below.

Freezing offer, warm heart

It wasn't just the larger brands either. The Drewe Arms is a pub in Exeter who stepped up to help the local community by baking and creating meals for them while raising money for charity.

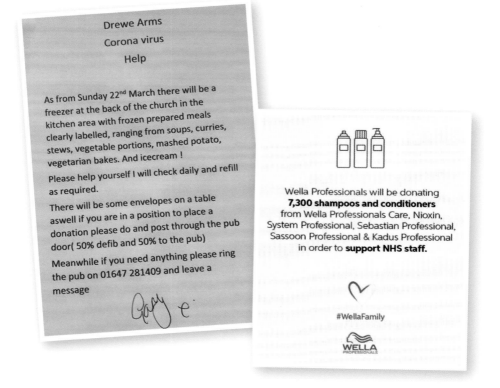

Drewe Arms

Corona virus

Help

As from Sunday 22nd March there will be a freezer at the back of the church in the kitchen area with frozen prepared meals clearly labelled, ranging from soups, curries, stews, vegetable portions, mashed potato, vegetarian bakes. And icecream !

Please help yourself I will check daily and refill as required.

There will be some envelopes on a table aswell if you are in a position to place a donation please do and post through the pub door(50% defib and 50% to the pub)

Meanwhile if you need anything please ring the pub on 01647 281409 and leave a message

Wella Professionals will be donating **7,300 shampoos and conditioners** from Wella Professionals Care, Nioxin, System Professional, Sebastian Professional, Sassoon Professional & Kadus Professional in order to **support NHS staff.**

#WellaFamily

WELLA
PROFESSIONALS

Visually stunning

One of the last events I did before we were all locked down was at the iconic Celtic Manor Resort in Wales. I was the closing speaker at the Vision Express annual conference. Just a few weeks later I was tagged into an extraordinary LinkedIn post by Danielle Hutchins, Store Manager in the Northampton store.

Had a call this morning from a lady who lives not too far from Vision Express in Evesham. Unfortunately one of her lenses had fallen out of her frame and her old specs were just not working as well. She is stuck in doors with her disabled husband and they haven't left the house since Covid-19 took over everyone's lives. So as simple as it might seem, I drove with my screwdriver, different size screws and PPE! To be greeted by her at the door and on the front step a box with her broken glasses in and a box of chocs! Simplest thing that store managers, optical assistants and optoms do on a daily basis in normal circumstances. She was delighted with the level of service and when I added that if there was any shopping she needed she was gobsmacked. I told her I had no issue at all delivering it after work and that she had my number if she needed it. I got into my car and wiped away a few tears. It's so heart-warming to go that little bit further. hashtag#celebrityservice is what Geoff Ramm spoke about at our conference and it has really stuck! The smallest of gestures mean the world to lots of people!

Royal stamp of approval

There is a reason I drive past three post offices to get to the West Boldon Post Office. You see it is run by a multi-award-winning husband and wife duo, Sean and Kate, who have quickly become the hub of the local community. They are also very active on social media, and on Facebook they decided to create a competition inviting children to design their very own stamp. Entries soon came flooding in. To the delight of local families, Sean and Kate posted a winner every day. And you wonder why I make a longer journey than strictly necessary when I post out my books and postcards?

Animals still need feeding

Chester Zoo was closed to visitors but that didn't stop them using their imagination to open their doors free of charge to everyone. With the aid of live streaming videos, children all over the world could access the entire zoo to see the animals being fed live, on the hour, every hour.

A shining example

Although the Village Hotel Wirral had to close, this didn't stop Tracy Colley from creating Celebrity Service for a couple of their team members. She posted images and the following message; 'We didn't want our General Manager and Maintenance Manager to feel too alone in that big hotel so we left them their very own handmade "Wilson", oh and a few other surprises!!'

Remote Ramm & Risner

During this time I personally made the decision to help as many clients as possible. Through podcasts, 'live sessions' (virtual keynotes) and radio interviews, as well as signing and sending out postcards to everyone.

However, one of my career highlights took place alongside my speaking partner in crime, Nigel Risner. He is not only a great friend but also a wonderful speaker. I was asked by a gentleman called Simon Briton from Quantify R&D if I would appear on a webinar to help raise money for Grace House children's charity. Businesses could log in, listen to my stories and ideas and then donate to help the charity. As you can imagine their vital fundraising efforts had come to an abrupt halt. I immediately said 'Yes, would love to'. I asked Nigel if he'd be involved too and his response was the same. So we got together one Friday afternoon to deliver our onstage double-act 'Perfect Day'. It is an energetic, fun session for businesses that we have delivered across the UK and Europe – this was the first time via a PC monitor. We raised over £1300 pounds – and counting, as most of the donations are recurring payments. To this day it is one of the greatest things we have done together.

Lockdown locks

Every day the stylists at Peter Mark created videos and posted them throughout their social channels offering hints, tips and advice on how to look after and style your hair.

NHS

I don't believe I could add anything else to those we all know who are the true heroes of this period. So rather than trying to find my own words, I present you with those of Sir Winston Churchill which apply just as much in 2020 as they did on the 29th October 1941... 'Never was so much owed by so many to so few.'

Captain – Colonel – Sir Tom

This section simply would not be complete without the name of one more person. Captain Tom Moore. The Second World War veteran, known to most as Captain Tom, aimed to raise £1000 for the NHS by completing 100 laps of his garden in Bedfordshire before his 100th birthday. What can I say? The nation and the world took him to their hearts. Captain Tom was left speechless as he raised more than £30 million for the National Health Service. On his 100th birthday over 125,000 cards were sent to him including one from the Duke and Duchess of Cambridge and the Duke hailed him as a 'one-man fundraising machine'. He also received a flypast from the Royal Air Force. Together with the whole world, I salute you Captain Tom, or, as you soon became, Colonel Tom. You raised funds, you lifted spirits and you won the hearts of the country.

I wrote a phrase during this time 'Be proud of what you achieved, in the time that you had'. Whether for you that meant looking after a neighbour, homeschooling your children, completing a Joe Wicks session without slipping a disc, clapping every Thursday night at 8 pm, staying in or going out on to the frontline, or simply surviving... just be proud of what you did.

In week one Hayley said to me, 'One day our grandchildren will ask us, "Grandma, Grandad, we are learning about Corona 2020 at school. What did you do during that time?"' We will say, 'We played, we learned and we did what we could.'

And I will take out the book you have in your hands right now and say 'I wrote this.'

Merry Summermas

When the world around you spins uncontrollably never lose focus on your clients and what they may be going through.

Some may say it was genius, others crazy, but this is what I did during the summer of 2020 to put a smile on my clients' faces.

With my clients pretty much frozen in time, I decided to deliver a piece of Celebrity Service magic. First up – I made a quick call to Father Christmas. (I have his direct number.) I wanted to tempt him out of semi-retirement six months early to bring some much needed joy. He agreed.

Since I started my own business in 2002 I've always sent gifts to those who have booked me, but why wait until December, especially this of all years? My clients need a boost now, I thought to myself.

So I changed the date of Christmas, bringing it forward to the 25th June. I designed Christmas cards and handpicked and packed (with the help of Grace) chocolate hampers.

The card read:

This year everything has turned upside down. It's not easy to keep track of the day, month or season. With this in mind I am bringing Christmas forward…

The other side is blank (for a handwritten personalised message).

The gifts:

Unfortunately, I couldn't buy festive goodies, but I figured a box full of chocs would still be exciting to open.

The response was phenomenal. The voicemails, emails, posts on social media and phone calls were wonderful. I could hear the smiles shining through. Well done, Santa and your face-masked reindeer!

Don't wait to create a greater client experience. Sometimes now is the best time to create a smile.

INTERVIEW

SIMON WHITAKER

MANAGING DIRECTOR

MASTER DEBONAIR

I have always loved my three-piece suits, but I have never had so many compliments since I started wearing a Master Debonair suit.

What is the greatest piece of service you've seen at Master Debonair?

" There's a customer, Andrew, he lost a lot of weight, but at the same time he also lost a lot of confidence. His brother brought him into the shop, so myself and Eve spent a couple hours with him. That was the first time that we had ever really given a personal shopping experience. We fitted everything and he just looked fantastic. We advised him on his size, we got him all tailored and everything shipped to him. He sent us a letter that said 'I can't thank you enough you've actually changed my life and my confidence so much. I've not had a partner or a girlfriend for years now but I've just started dating again.' This is now quite a regular thing at Master Debonair, where we get people who walk out with confidence. Our strapline has become 'Outfitting self-confidence'. And that's what it's all about. The product is just a by-product. The products are given. The service is everything.

What is YOUR number one customer service superpower?

I will take the time needed to speak to customers directly.

I still keep my eye on our business social feeds as well. So now and again, if I see anything, I'll reply personally. We get so much traction and engagement that people don't expect a reply, but I reply to everything where I can and I don't give standard replies. Everything is tailored to what they've asked and the different situations.

We will do everything that we humanly can to make sure that the customer feels great and has the best experience. And we don't get it right all the time. Nobody can. But then it's about how you deal with that as well.

So my superpower is taking the time with people, whether that's customers or staff.

What three things can any business or organisation do right now to create a greater Celebrity Service experience?

1. Know your customer inside out regardless of how many customers you've got.

2. Admit when you are wrong and put things right.

3. Gestures don't need to be grand, just small and personal.

What examples can you share of how you or your team deliver a greater internal experience?

Check in on people and ask them how they are. Sometimes you can get into work and everything can be going at a million miles an hour, but we don't know what kind of day the staff member or the customer has had or how they've woken up, so it's important to keep asking them. I want everybody at Master Debonair to look out for everybody else as well. I know we've all got the day-to-day things going on, but sometimes people are struggling and you can't really tell, so it's important to ask and really try to help.

What infuriates you most about customer service or the lack of?

If I walk into any kind of shop, it doesn't matter who the person is, age, gender, whatever, and I can see they're clearly not interested, that drives me nuts. It's something that we don't tolerate at MD. As soon as somebody walks in here the guys will ask 'Where have you travelled from? Do you need a drink or do you need the toilet first?' When you walk into places and the staff are clearly not interested, I think that says a lot about the brand.

If you had a magic wand what would you wave it over to instantly ensure a greater service is delivered?

It would be the understanding of how you make that first impression, whether it's via body language or whatever comes out of your mouth straight away. Not everybody's the same and that's the beauty of having different staff. We've got different ages, genders, backgrounds – they're all very different. What I don't want is everybody to be the same as me. God forbid. But if I could wave that wand, it would be for everyone to think about what they're going to say first. From getting up in the morning, you know those first words with your other half, your kids, your dog, the postman, whoever, can all of a sudden set your day straight away. Think about what you're going to say and how you're going to react straight away. This world would just be a phenomenal place if everyone did that.

THE GREATER
GOOD

In this chapter you will meet some of those extraordinary individuals and businesses who provide a great customer experience for people whose names they don't even know. They spot the opportunity to help those who need it, treating them with the Celebrity Service touch without any expectation of return or gain.

Saving people and planet

When I see the colour purple, I see Cadbury. While browsing their sumptuous shelves of cocoa heaven I came across a wonderful campaign for the greater good.

The chocolate bars we all know and love were right there in front of my eyes. But there was something missing. It was the words.
The lack of copy on the packaging drew me in and I needed to find out why.

Cadbury and their iconic Dairy Milk bar had teamed up with Age UK to tackle the loneliness of older people. Beside the chocolate bars the following message was displayed:

> *The words have been 'donated' to AGE UK to help the 225,000 older people who regularly go without speaking to anyone for a whole week.*

> *Cadbury will donate 30p to the charity for every limited edition bar sold.*

One million bars were sold with £300,000 donated to the charity. On top of the cash the campaign also achieved a greater awareness of the need for all of us to reach out to older people who might be suffering from loneliness.

While walking down Bank Street in Newquay, I noticed another greater good sign: a poster in a window demonstrating how Rowe's Cornish Bakers are helping to reduce the addition to landfill of single-use plastics. They do this by inviting passers-by to use the free water refill service in their store.

The Oyster Box in Durban, South Africa, encourages their guests to look after the local environment. For every bucket of rubbish collected at the beach you will receive a free cocktail or milkshake. They even supply the buckets for you.

rowe's
CORNISH BAKERS

WE WILL REFILL
YOUR WATER BOTTLE
FOR FREE.

JUST ASK A MEMBER OF
STAFF.

The Oyster Box

GET YOUR **FREE DRINK**
(COCKTAIL OR MILKSHAKE)

...WHEN YOU COLLECT
A BUCKET OF RUBBISH OFF
THE BEACH.

BUCKETS AVAILABLE FROM BEACH GATE GUARD
Full buckets to be returned to reception to redeem your voucher
(HOTEL RESIDENTS ONLY • TERMS & CONDITIONS APPLY)

LEADING
HOTELS

Jamie and his technicolour dreamcoats

You know you are about to meet someone special when everyone in the business mentions them to you before you even arrive for your visit. Hearing his story and the impact it's had, you can't help but be inspired.

I had the pleasure of meeting Jamie Hunter at a conference, shaking his hand while passing him two big black liners full of winter coats.

He's a national account manager at Village Hotels. He is also a volunteer for an organisation called Burton Hope, a small local charity helping the vulnerable and homeless.

I caught up with him again to share his story and his passion, which I hope will inspire you and your business too.

'There's this lady and her name is Donna. She's in her late 50s. I just got chatting to her every week when I went to Sainsbury's in the local town where I currently live. She was sitting outside and she's homeless. I ended up doing my shopping but buying an extra meal deal and passing it to her as I walked outside. I sat down beside her and we just got chatting. She is just such a lovely, lovely lady.

'Like many of us, I've always tried to do my bit for charity. But meeting Donna got me thinking. I'd never seen anything out there to raise money or create something on a bigger scale for homeless people.'

Jamie wanted to help and with a Google search found Burton Hope, close to his home.

After spending some time on the streets handing out food he had an idea. As the nights were becoming darker and colder, his idea was to collect winter coats to give to the homeless people of Burton.

'We all have a coat or two in the back of our wardrobes that we no longer wear. I could simply put a post on Facebook and invite friends and family to donate a coat. My goal was to collect 500.'

When hearing of his idea at work his sales director, the marketing team and 31 Village Hotels rallied behind him to support his campaign as part of their Village Green Initiative.

The campaign was branded #hopeforacoat And the bar had been set a little higher… to collect 1000 winter coats in just five weeks.

Jamie added, 'I was delighted Village were as passionate as I was about making a real difference. First of all we created the brand and then we issued a challenge to every hotel to create a space in their foyer to raise awareness with both staff and our guests. The hotels love a bit of a healthy competition with each other.

'We set the general managers a task of creating a drop-off point in each hotel, because in my mind, the more quirky and creative the drop-off point was in relation to people living on the streets in the UK, the more it would make the public think when they come and bring that coat to us. We had a tent erected in Village Portsmouth. There was a weathered shed in Village Coventry. Everyone made a fantastic creative effort to engage. The general managers also reached out to their own local homeless charities to offer their coats to them. My jaw was on the floor as I saw everyone exceeding my expectations.

'For the entirety of the five-week campaign more than 4000 staff members were buzzing and excited. The awareness of what we were doing and the lovely people we were doing it for was inspiring.'

Lynn Fraser, sales director of Village Hotels added, 'Every Wednesday night Jamie would go to Greggs and buy umpteen meal deals and go round giving them out to the homeless in Burton. He also took round his friend who was a hairdresser to give people haircuts to make them feel better. We knew this was important to Jamie and as a business we wanted to support him.

'We also asked our corporate clients to support us by sharing and collecting too, which was quite remarkable. It was a real hearts and minds emotional campaign and something that didn't cost anything.

'Jamie will sit down, talk, find out about people on the street and take an interest. This is what differentiates him. He is one of my account managers, but he's also my best friend and I am very lucky.'

So the target was 500, and then 1000 and the final total was 21,110.

Yes, that's twenty-one thousand, one hundred and ten coats.

'We simply had too many coats!' Jamie beamed. 'So I called up a contact at the Ministry of Sound in London as they were doing their big homeless day charity event and I offered them the remaining coats. I hired a huge long-based truck and drove right into the centre of London to deliver them personally.

'I am very excited at the opportunity to be in your book, Geoff. I hope this highlights to everyone that when working collectively people can achieve so much and put so many smiles on so many faces. For over 21,000 homeless people it meant a warm, clean coat for the winter. And I hope it does inspire people. You just have to think of what you can do, because after all it's a bit of effort. It doesn't need to cost anything. Look at me. I had that little idea and look what it turned into.

'You know, if we all come together... well, it's the old saying. You drop a pebble into an ocean...'

Sleighdium of Light

It is said that Coca Cola changed the colour of Christmas. In keeping with their brand colours, they turned the emerald green tones of Santa Claus, into red and white.

Personally I believe in the magic of Christmas and that deep down Santa Claus has always been a Sunderland fan. But we may never know. On the subjects of Santa, Sunderland, Christmas and a time of giving, there was one festive game that had a huge impact on the community and the city.

On Boxing Day, 2018, Sunderland were due to play Bradford City. Christmas is a time when many fans living away from the area will return to their native North East to visit their families. As the football fixtures come thick and fast in December, fans returning home for the festivities will often attend a game that they would not normally be around for.

In the months leading up to the Boxing Day match there was a sense of optimism that my beloved club could set a new record for the highest ever attendance for a League One game. The record currently held by Leeds United at 38,256.

Myself, Hayley, Grace and Elliot donned our hats, scarfs and gloves and made our way to the stadium. We witnessed first hand our club smashing the record, as 46,039 fans entered the Stadium of Light. A 1-0 win was much needed. However, the game will also be remembered for one piece of Celebrity Service for the greater good of fellow supporters.

One season card holder, Simon Baty, came up with a wonderful initiative called 'Gift of Football' that united both the city and local community, ensuring a Christmas to remember for many fans. He encouraged the club, fellow supporters and the local business community to consider buying an extra ticket for those less fortunate.

An amazing 1,650 extra tickets were purchased by supporters, staff, players and local businesses. The tickets were donated to those fans who couldn't afford a ticket at this most expensive time of the year.

For as long as I can remember Sunderland has always been called 'The Caring Club'. They have always reached out and supported schools, charities and the wider community. It's a special place where the heart, passion and devotion are unsurpassed in England. Simon's 'Gift of Football' initiative continues every Christmas and Santa still wears his red and white colours with pride.

One person, one idea, helping many.

Backbone of the community

My local chiropractor isn't very local. Every month I travel up the A19 motorway, go through the Tyne Tunnel and once through the other side, a further 20 minute drive will see me arrive at the coastal town of Tynemouth. I make this longer than necessary journey because they are brilliant. They care. They always fit me in (even on weekends or out of hours when my spine decides to lock). I am then adjusted by either Estelle or a member of her team at Naturally Chiropractic.

But towards the end of the year, around early November time, the adjustment rooms start to grow. Every hour of every day the room starts to fill with toys, dolls, games, jigsaws, board games and yes, even more toys.

'In our very first year in business (2005) I remember myself and my practice manager Claire looking out the window on a cold dark late afternoon, looking towards the beach, waiting for our next client to arrive. I turned to Claire and said "We need to do something to make the world feel better and to support our community.

'Although we were very new in business and are just a small practice, I wanted to give back. It's a small community we live in and with Christmas coming up I said why don't we create 'A Toy For Adjustment' day. It is something I have seen in Australia, but never here in the UK.' (Estelle is originally from Albury.)

Estelle and her team of chiropractors donated one day of their time, adjusting their clients in exchange for a toy.

'The first couple of years all of the toys we collected were donated to the local hospital in North Tyneside. In fact we collected so many toys they had excess to give away for an additional two years. But they then told us the Freeman Hospital in Newcastle who were struggling so we took a van load to them too.

'The funny thing is most clients who donate don't actually have an appointment on the day itself. They just love the idea, they loved to be involved. It became their local campaign too.

'Momentum was really building in the first few years, to the extent where our clients would start to ask about 'Toys For Adjustment' Day as early as August.

'The following year we approached our local radio station, Metro, to help boost their 'Cash For Kids' campaign. The guy who was running it burst into tears when I pulled up in a car full of toys, followed by a transit van, oh and then another car. Toys were distributed throughout the entire region, in time for Santa squeezing down the chimney.

'A few years ago we decided to bring our focus back into the immediate local area and approached the Salvation Army. At the same time one of our clients runs a local 'food bank', so we also started collecting food as well as the toys.'

Naturally Chiropractic are without doubt the backbone of the community. Tens of thousands of toys, games, puzzles, dolls and food items have been collected since they started. But a greater good idea wouldn't remain in the local community for long.

Estelle added, 'I introduced the 'Toys For Adjustment' concept to the United Chiropractic Association in association with the Trussell Trust and for the last 10 years chiropractors have adopted the day and have been Adjusting For Toys across the country.

'What started out as an idea looking out onto the beach, on a cold dark afternoon, has helped children and families in need which is something we are so proud of.'

The greater good is about seeing the opportunity to help those close to you. But by involving your customers or clients to donate, share, help and support, you never know, you could see what looks like a local ripple, turn into a nationwide wave.

INTERVIEW

JOANNA SWASH

CEO

CALL ANSWERING SERVICE MONEYPENNY

When I first visited Moneypenny I was bowled over by their ideas and attention to detail (so much so I dedicated six pages to them in Celebrity Service). We are clients of each other.

What is the greatest piece of service you've seen at Moneypenny?

" One day, we took a call and it was from the child of one of our clients. They were stuck outside their school having tried to ring their parents but couldn't get hold of them. So the child phoned their business number saying, 'Where are you, Dad? I need picking up.' Our PA, Kathy, had taken the call and she chose to stay on the phone with the child while her colleague phoned every number we'd ever had for the parents until we got hold of one of them. They each thought the other was picking up their child. It's all about doing the right thing at the right time.

What is the right thing? Everyone has complete freedom to do the right thing. You can't train for that. It was just going totally above and beyond. So that is the memory that gives me the spine tingles because Kathy did the right thing. It was winter, so it was dark but she kept the child talking while they waited for the parents to get there.

What infuriates you most about customer service or the lack of?

Being treated like a number rather than a person. For example, if somebody asks, 'What's your account number?' I want to reply 'You could just have my name'. Why do they need an account number? The client doesn't know their account number, but they know their own name! So just ask them for that.

People who are late. That just shows a lack of thought about what other people have got going on in their lives.

A bad attitude. We want to surround ourselves with people with a great attitude who are radiators of positivity even when they're not feeling particularly positive.

Breaking promises. If you're going to make a promise, keep it. You don't have to make it in the first place. You know, no one's forced you. If you know you're going to break a promise, go and explain why this actually won't work out any more and just be honest and open.

If you had a magic wand what would you wave it over to instantly ensure a greater service is delivered

I think one thing all businesses would like is to have more time. If you had all the time in the world, you would be able to concentrate on just one thing at a time. You would then move on and do the next thing brilliantly too and it wouldn't matter how long it took you. Time enables you to be a better version of yourself. It enables you to plan better.

What is YOUR number one customer service superpower?

Wearing our customers' shoes.

When Ed and Rachel first started the business, they said, 'If I was a client, what would I need? And if I was a member of the team, how would I want to be treated?' We always try very hard to wear our customers' shoes. That involves real thinking about how it feels to be part of that business and their needs. What are the challenges? What is it like to be on your own and trying to set up a business? What does it feel like to hand your baby (your business telephone lines and Live Chat) over to somebody else to look after all your incoming calls and chats? Would you go and give your mobile to some random stranger in the street and say, 'There you go, you can answer that for the afternoon. I'll see you later.'?

Loyalty comes out of that as well. If somebody truly feels understood then you've created a really loyal customer base, because it's all about relationships. Understanding somebody fully helps to create a really great relationship, whether that's in your personal life or whether that's from a work perspective.

So, wearing your customers' shoes, understanding how it feels to be them, creating a great relationship and then loyalty comes out the other end.

What examples can you share of how you or your team deliver a greater internal experience?

1. We treat everybody like a celebrity.

   Anybody who walks into the business is a celebrity. It's one of the reasons why we don't have dedicated parking spaces, because actually everybody who walks into the business, whether it's a visitor or a client, a prospect or a member of the team, they are all celebrities.

2. We trust people.

   So for us, that means no scripts; Clients let us represent them because they know we put trust at the heart of everything we do and that we give our brilliant people the tools to do a great job. When they lend us the keys to their business, our people treat it like our own. We never let them down. We make them shine.

3. We create relationships.

   It's not a process. Service is delivered by human beings who want to do the right thing. Mindful that each client is different we adapt with them as their needs change, whether in person, over the phone or through tech, we bring warmth, individual personality and a smile to every conversation.

INTERVIEW

NOEL LORD

HEAD OF RETAIL SALES AND CHANNEL DEVELOPMENT

METLIFE INSURANCE, AUSTRALIA
HE IS ALSO THE FOUNDER OF CARE 360

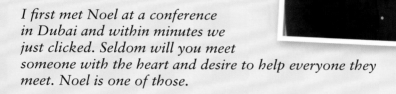

I first met Noel at a conference in Dubai and within minutes we just clicked. Seldom will you meet someone with the heart and desire to help everyone they meet. Noel is one of those.

What is the greatest piece of service you've seen?

" Great client service starts with a mindset that encourages innovation and continuous improvement within the business and a safe environment to allow people to 'fail'. That way they become confident to try new things.

When I worked at Macquerie, I recall an elderly client – a grandmother who needed to withdraw funds to make a significant purchase as a surprise. She was buying her granddaughter a car as she had just got her licence.

The staff member processed the transaction, but the cheque was sent to the wrong address, as the client had moved residence and not advised us. The client rang back asking where the cheque was. Today was the day she needed to buy the car.

When the staff member realised what had happened, she took it upon herself to come up with a solution that delivered a great client experience. She created a new cheque and in her lunch break got a cab to the client's house with the cheque so that the client could surprise her granddaughter with the car purchase that afternoon.

What is YOUR number one customer service superpower?

We all judge others by their impact, but we judge ourselves on our intent. If we can change this we can be focused on each interaction and the impact we have creates a great environment for client service delivery.

What three things can any business or organisation do right now to create a greater Celebrity Service experience?

1. Foster an environment of continuous improvement.

2. Really focus on creating a growth mindset in the business, which means 'freedom within boundaries', allowing people to fail safely. Then you will find they are prepared to implement new ideas and change and you will really see innovation in service.

3. Always focus on our impact not our intent.

What examples can you share of how you or your team deliver a greater internal experience?

Creating a framework to grow our people and sales will grow as a result.

We have created a programme that provides our sales teams and management with a structure that they can follow that provides focus, discipline and accountability to their role, and allows them to adapt to their own style within a framework that provides time for planning and also time for reflection.

I call it the STAR Sales Programme, which is an acronym for Sales, Target, Activity, Result.

So in our planning we use STAR and in our review we use RATS, which is STAR in reverse.

Planning – STAR

What am I selling? Clearly articulating in my own thoughts what I am selling.

Who is my target? Who am I trying to sell to?

What is my planned activity? How will I go about this, is it face to face or by telephone or some other way?

What result am I looking to achieve? Every meeting needs an outcome and this outcome needs to be thought through and recorded beforehand.

Reviewing – RATS

Did I get the right result? By having a focus on the desired result I can ensure I stay focused on what I am trying to achieve.

Through the right activity? This helps me identify what activities get me the best results.

To the right target? Am I speaking to the right people to progress?

With the right sales message? Was I clear enough about what it was I was selling?

This programme is designed to create a framework that allows sales people to own it so they can apply their own approach within a structured framework.

We have embedded this into our CRM, which keeps it real and live for the business.

I use the term 'get on the balcony and off the dance floor', spend time on your business not always in your business. The key for this programme is to develop our sales people to think as if it's their business, and they are not just employees; they can take some ownership within appropriate boundaries.

What infuriates you most about customer service or the lack of?

I get really frustrated when I see businesses that have no interest in improving. I see that as arrogance in so far as they believe they can't improve or they are already the best. This is like swimming naked in a high tide; you only get exposed when things change.

I also get infuriated when I see staff spending their time 'bagging' the opposition to clients and prospects. This tells me they are more focused on external things they can't control and not what they can change internally.

If you had to place a customer service star along Hollywood Boulevard, whose name would be on it?

Cam Pearse from Pearse Footwear, Brisbane.

Cam owns a family business that imports footwear and accessories from all over the world to Australia and provides these to stores to sell to the public. He had a client in Far North Queensland who was facing some domestic challenges. She had taken in a young man, a friend of her son, who had tragically lost his parents. He was 13 and with little prospect of a normal life until this lady decided to bring him into her family. However, this created some financial pressures for this client and her business. Hearing about this, Cam and Pearse Footwear decided they would go above and beyond to assist, so Cam decided to run a golf day from which all the funds raised would go to the young 13 year old and therefore remove some of the financial pressure his client was experiencing.

Over $25K was raised from the golf day and the auctions held.

This was not driven by a focus on making more sales from his client. It was all about helping and having the most significant positive impact he could for his client.

YOU
REMEMBERED

One of the oldest tricks in the customer experience playbook is memory. Remembering someone's name, their likes, their loves or simply remembering an occasion or a time of year... here are four great examples that stand out...

It's always time for chocolate

We visited the medieval city of York one Saturday to meet up with some friends. It was a scorcher of a day and the ice creams were aplenty. We didn't want the day to end so instead of driving home that night we decided to stay the night and we booked in at the York Pavilion Hotel.

This was the first time Grace had stayed outside of our home since she was born. At 10 months old, Grace was an early riser – and I am talking anytime from 4.30 am onwards. Regardless of how many blackout blinds we could install to help her sleep through to a 'normal' hour, nothing really worked.

So here we are in the hotel. Hayley and I know our little bundle of joy will awake early and when she does we'll leap out of bed, mix the milk, get dressed, walk around the streets of York waiting for the sun to rise and then head back for breakfast.

Right on cue at precisely 4:47 am Grace awoke. By 5:35 am we were ready to leave the room and go for a stroll.

I opened the door.

There by my feet was a large Mars Bar Easter egg. It was Easter Sunday. We had totally forgotten. When you are a new parent, dates, times, and occasions do tend to slip. Wow!

As I reached down to pick it up I noticed another egg outside the room next door and then another and another. Every hotel guest had an egg placed outside of their door. How thoughtful. They remembered it was Easter and given everyone a gift. This wonderful customer experience would only have cost a couple of pounds per hotel room.

Checkout was very busy that morning so we popped the key in the box and left.

A week later the chocolate egg had disappeared but the memory of this experience was still fresh in my mind. So I rang the hotel and asked to speak to the manager.

'Speaking,' came the reply.

'Oh, hello my name is Geoff Ramm, we stayed with you last Saturday evening.'

'Er, yeees?' came the reply, filled with nervous wondering.

'I thought the idea of an Easter egg surprise outside everyone's door last Sunday was amazing. As a speaker I love to share real-life examples with audiences to help inspire them. So would you mind if I used your hotel as a wonderful example?'

She was blown away. Then she shared a sad truth with me. I was the only person to have thanked them. Even worse... she added that two guests had actually complained.

The complaints that Easter Sunday morning were about religious beliefs and dietary requirements leading to the chocolate egg not being appreciated.

You cannot please everyone.

But what she said next will stay with me forever.

'I was going to stop doing this because of those two complaints. But because of your call to say how amazing the idea was, we will keep doing it.'

Have you any idea how many people I have told this story to?

Here are some things to consider:

Remember important dates.

If it feels like the right thing to do, do it.

Not everyone will love your thoughtful ideas.

When you receive a great Celebrity Service, don't keep it to yourself. Tell the business, tell the individual, either right there and then, or wait a week and give them a call. It might just make all the difference to whether they carry on being Superstars or they give up because of a lack of appreciation.

Home sweet home

People will often say that moving house is one of the most stressful things you can do in your lifetime. And of course they're right.

However, at the outset, it is all rather lovely. You spend your Sunday evenings trawling through estate agents' websites. Clicking on the house that takes your fancy, then clicking and scrolling further to take a sneak peek into each room.

You draw up a short list of those you wish to view and then you make the appointment.

Right at this moment it's rather exciting. You go and view the house and then you either get back in your car and cross it off because it didn't tick all your boxes or you have found the perfect place for you and your family for the next stage of your lives.

It's a good idea to always try to remember to bottle this level of excitement as it's probably not going to last.

You agree to buy the home of your dreams. You have a buyer for your home.

In order to get to this point and to get those keys to your new house in your hand there's going to be a lot of different people and businesses introduced into the mix, and with that comes an awful lot of communications.

And this, ladies and gentlemen, is where the fun begins…

Financial advisors – can we afford this property?

Solicitors – who can we trust to ensure everyone is where they need to be legally?

Estate agents – who will you choose to represent the sale of your current home?

Removal firms – who is available on the day? What will they include, for example boxes and/or packing?

If you've ever moved quickly and had the experience of everyone doing what they said they'd do and doing it on time – well then – everyone deserves a medal. In our three house moves to date, efficiency and great communication are not things you'd associate with the event or the people that work in this sector.

Rather than go into each and every detail (believe me the book would be triple the size), let me cut to the chase and go straight to moving in day. The keys are in my hand and I'm unlocking the door into the next phase of my family's life while I reveal to you what happened. (Or didn't.)

The Government

Stamp duty is paid on the property, which the UK Government take. It would have been nice to hear from them. Maybe a thank you email or perhaps a letter, but nothing. In all honesty, we'd never expect anything really. Yet stamp duty is the highest bill of the lot in the moving process, so perhaps some piece of communication from them, for example, 'This is what your duty has gone towards: NHS, policing, schools, etc.', would make this a less bitter pill to swallow.

Estate agents

The second highest fee paid is to the estate agents. While our agent was lovely and very efficient (we'd used them 12 years previously), on moving day there was no card, no flowers, no wine, no chocolate, basically no thanks, gratitude or small gift to say 'thank you' 'good luck' or 'welcome to your new home'. It was sad to remember that they used to do this. But they stopped. Why?

Solicitors

Despite being only 17 miles away we never actually met face to face. All communications and correspondence were via email, phone call or post. But they did know our moving date (after all they were the ones that gave it to us). On moving day there was no card, no flowers, no wine, no chocolate, basically no thanks, gratitude or a small gift to say 'thank you' 'good luck' or 'welcome to your new home'. Celebrity Service opportunity lost forever.

Removal firm

Two large vans and six men who worked tirelessly to empty our old home and to then fill our new one. The only thing that worked as hard as them on moving day was our kettle. However, in between emptying one house and waiting outside the new house for the go-ahead from us via the solicitor and estate agent, the teams sat in their vans for over six hours. Six whole hours to buy a card, pick up some flowers or wine or some chocolate (at least for the kids). No. Nothing again, no thanks or gratitude or a small gift to say 'thank you' 'good luck' or 'welcome to your new home'.

Financial advisors

Last but not least were the financial advisors, or to give them a greater billing, Michael Tweddle and his team from Instinct Financial Solutions. On moving day we received a card from the whole team. We also received a beautifully wrapped gift box. Inside was a tea caddy, tea and two china cups and a note welcoming us to our new home. What is most impressive is that of all the fees we paid out, theirs was the smallest. And we had only really dealt with them at the very beginning, some eight months prior to moving. Stunning.

Right now your products and services could also be in amongst a chain of companies working with your customer. Why not be the one that delivers more, thinks more and acts more than the rest?

If I were in charge of any of these businesses I'd have ordered a thousand branded 'new home' cards, just ready to be personally signed and sent. It costs pennies, but means the world. You could have also gone one stage further and gone online to send a personalised card, after all you know the names of the family members!

They say home is where your heart is, but is your heart truly in the right place – where the customer can have the best experience of it?

Something in cider so strong

I am fortunate to both work and play in the South West of England. The Great Western Train journey from London Paddington to the land of the scone (cream first, jam second/jam first, cream second – it's all good with me) is one of the best there is.

The adjoining counties of Devon and Cornwall are a tourism magnet for holidaymakers from across the UK and indeed the world. And I have long believed the people born here have a rich service culture running through their veins. It's why I have so many stories and examples of businesses and individuals from this region who appreciate and live the Celebrity Service philosophy.

One of these businesses is Larkbeare Grange, a stunning country house bed and breakfast, near Exeter. When I first met and stayed with Charlie, Julia and Joanna, if truth be known, I had never had a breakfast like it.

All home grown or locally sourced produce: the eggs, the jams, the butter, the freshly squeezed juice, bacon, bread fresh out of the Aga… amazing. It seriously set me up for my West Country Tourism Conference later that morning. Charlie even dropped me off at the venue!

Fast forward two years and I was on my way back. Not only for the conference the next day but also returning to stay at Larkbeare

Grange. I was dreaming of the breakfast even on the evening train journey down – it couldn't come soon enough. I met Julia and Charlie once again and they gave me a key to my room. Putting my laptop case to the side and hanging up my suit I noticed a postcard and two gifts on the bureau.

Oh my, they remembered!

Two years previously I mentioned on stage that one of my favourite drinks was cider – more specifically Rattler cider, which is brewed in Cornwall.

It was like I'd died and gone to Devon.

You are too thoughtful

I hopped on the last flight from Newcastle to Southampton. I arrived on the south coast at 11 pm and made my way to Portsmouth in a taxi. At around 20 minutes to midnight I got to the Village Hotel, Portsmouth.

I checked in, took the lift up and started searching for my room, number 425. Despite it being at the very end of the corridor I could see it. This wasn't through memory (it was my first time here) and it wasn't a lucky guess. I could see that the room way off into the distance was mine.

With my hand luggage behind me I started to smile as I walked. The smile increased in width until I arrived at the door where I now was laughing. Here we are, room 425. I placed my key card against the door and entered my room. There on the bed the thoughtfulness continued, but not just for me, there was something for Hayley, for Grace and for Elliot too.

But here is the most surprising part of this situation… I wasn't here to work with the hotel and their team. I wasn't even here to run a session in the hotel for another client. In fact, the client I was speaking for at a different venue the next day had simply booked the hotel. All they had done was give them my name.

Some months previously, Michael Horner the general manager of the hotel had attended one of my sessions at the Village GM Conference. And he remembered. He remembered my interests, he remembered my football team, he remembered the names of my nearest and dearest.

Michael must have spotted my name (there aren't too many of us) and with his team created an unbelievable Celebrity Service experience, just for me.

What do you know about your customer's likes, loves, passions and interests? When you find out, log them in your mind or add them to your CRM system. Then you too can surprise and delight someone with Superstar treatment as Michael did for me.

INTERVIEW

SARAH GASKIN

HEAD CONCIERGE

THE HEADLAND HOTEL AND SPA,
CORNWALL

*Sarah has an unrivalled
passion for her place of work,
The Headland Hotel and Spa and the county
of Cornwall. She recently received her Golden Keys and became a
part of the Les Clefs d'Or society. She is a wonderful lady who I
have not only had the pleasure of working alongside, but as a family
we have been on the receiving end of her Celebrity Service. She
takes a genuine interest in people, gets a kick out of achieving the
'impossible' and does it all with a great sense of humour.*

What is YOUR number one customer service superpower?

"I am genuinely interested in people. I will make you feel like
you have come home when you arrive at the hotel and that you're
not just another paying guest. I will welcome you as a friend, not a
stranger. Every guest counts, young, old and those with four legs!
They're not just visitors or guests they're potential friends for life.
There's no better feeling than to know you've made someone's day.
I'm persistent and never accept second best...

What three things can any business or organisation do right now to create a greater Celebrity Service experience?

1. Recruit people with the right attitude because you can train skills
   but you can't train attitude.

2. Recognise and reward employees who are passionate about
   excellent service and shout about them so people understand
   what you want everyone to achieve.

3. Let your team have a guest experience so they understand what great customer service feels like.

If you had a magic wand what would you wave it over to instantly ensure a greater service is delivered?

Consistently excellent service throughout the whole hotel 24/7.

What infuriates you most about customer service or the lack of?

1. Lack of passion for customer service – you are employed to do a job, do it well.

2. Being ignored – a guest or customer is the most important person in the workplace, to ignore them is a failure and discourteous. We all like to be acknowledged and feel we matter.

3. Lack of attention to detail.

If you had to place a customer service star along Hollywood Boulevard, whose name would be on it?

Mr and Mrs Armstrong, the owners of the hotel. They really are the ultimate unsung Celebrity Service Superstars. They have looked after, nourished and grown the hotel for over 42 years and have made it what it is today. Without them and their passion and commitment to providing the very best guest experience possible and, of course, their continued investment and upgrading of the hotel we would not be the 5-star hotel that we are!

INTERVIEW

ALASDAIR SMITH

CHIEF EXECUTIVE
SCOTTISH BAKERS

Scottish Bakers have been supporting and protecting the interests of Scotland's bakery trade for over 125 years. They advise, train, support and deliver events to 200 members throughout the country.

" We represent 200 bakers across Scotland. The honesty of the trade is something that I just love. We often joke about bakers having flour in their veins because it is something that they do out of passion. You do not become a baker by accident or because there are no other options, you become a baker because you love the process and you love the output and you love producing something really beautiful out of something really quite humble.

What is the greatest piece of service you've seen at Scottish Bakers?

Let's take the Scottish Bakers training team... when we start speaking to a business about delivering apprenticeships, it's always about the business. We'll sit down with the business and we'll speak to them about what they want to achieve. We'll get an understanding of the workflow within the business. Of course, these businesses often don't work 9 to 5. If somebody wants to see us at night, the training team will go in on a night shift.

They will put on the whites and roll up their sleeves and get on the machines or the mixers with the clients and the trainees in place. For the time that they're on the premises, they become an additional resource and a part of that team. So we get to know the businesses that we work with inside out. We see great results for the traineeships, consistently getting completion rates way above the national averages for Scotland, England or Northern Ireland.

Good customer service is about always listening to what your customers are saying. And if there is some way in which you can deliver what they're asking for, then you should just do it.

What is YOUR number one customer service superpower?

I just talk to people.

It's all too easy to hide behind an email. I will pick up the phone and speak to someone. I like to understand what makes people tick. I'd like to feel that I've got some empathy with how they are feeling, what their pressures are, what their challenges are or what their ambitions might be. My job is to try and make sure they've got a way in which they can progress. So I don't consider I have a particular superpower, I just talk. I've spent my career talking for a living.

What is the greatest customer service experience you've ever received?

A couple of years ago, myself, my wife and my son, had a short break in Split, Croatia.

Split is a very busy place for cruise liners. There are waves and waves of tourists who breeze into this little square, get a cup of coffee, take pictures, it's heaving. We sat down on these stone steps outside the café. It was maybe about nine in the morning and the waiter came over and we just got chatting. We went off, had a lovely day in Split and then returned to the same café at around ten o'clock that night. The same waiter came over and said, 'Two Americanos and a cappuccino is it?' Amazing. A full day of tourists nonstop and he remembered our order.

What three things can any business or organisation do right now to create a greater Celebrity Service experience?

1. Be clear about what it is that you're looking to achieve. If you don't know what it is you're just going to be flopping around forever, so get real clarity, have a plan from the outset.

2. Be honest with yourself, because nobody gets it right all the time. So accept when things aren't right. If you can't make them right straight away then look at how you can make them better. Because sometimes, you know, that change has to happen incrementally.

3. I'm going to come back to that theme of talking. Unless you're communicating the first two things – what it is you want to achieve and what your challenges are in your business to improve – then you won't get either of those two done either. So the three are inextricably linked.

What infuriates you most about customer service or the lack of?

It's indifference.

It's the polar opposite of that example from the waiter in Split. It's going into a coffee shop and finding six of the tables are covered with dirty crockery. And there are a couple of people behind the counter, checking their phones. It's that indifference that you could find in any organisation, an office or a retail store, a café or a restaurant or even a service business like ours.

So, yeah, indifference, I think is the absolute enemy of trade.

If you had to place a customer service star along Hollywood Boulevard, whose name would be on it?

Scott Anderson (Scottish Baker's Training and Quality Manager). He pushes me and I think that's the right thing to do. Scott eats, sleeps and breathes the baking industry and has done since he was in his teens. If you sliced him open flour would spill out. Everything he does in his job is for the benefit of our membership and for the businesses that he deals with. He does it with such ferocious loyalty. He has to challenge me quite hard, which is right, you know, because I don't know about that kind of detail at the grassroots level. He's got a pretty good radar that I trust implicitly. He is someone who gives his all and will continue giving his all to the best of his ability, keeping his team motivated under huge pressure.

120
CHALLENGE

A SPORTY STAY

You came through the first 120 Challenge with magical flying colours (see page 59). But that was just one idea delivered via one touchpoint.

Now it's time to up the ante.

What if I were to say you could go on to create an incredible experience across dozens of customer touchpoints, and all within the same 120 seconds? I've been told on many occasions that it can't be done or that it is near impossible. However, the answers from every audience and team I've ever worked with will quickly dispel this notion.

This will really focus your combined efforts in generating Celebrity Service moments from start to finish. Using the same 120 technique, the same amount of people in your teams and with pen and paper to hand, here is your next challenge.

We are going to think about…

Hotels.

We've all stayed in them whether for work or pleasure, for one or two nights and for one- or two-week holidays. We're all accustomed to the check-in procedure, settling into the room, going for breakfast, enjoying an evening meal, a relaxing sleep and then checking out.

For this challenge you and your teams are going to create your very own hotel brand together with a jaw-dropping guest experience. However, this isn't any ordinary hotel. You are going to create a themed hotel. And the theme is sport.

Before your 120 second start, choose a sport, any sport… football, cricket, gymnastics, baseball, horse racing, rugby, basketball, netball, swimming or maybe something else.

Now write your chosen sport down on your piece of paper.

The Challenge

From check-in to check out, create a memorable experience at every single guest touchpoint. The winning team will be the one who has the longest list. We are after quantity here, not just quality. Here are 28 touchpoints (you can also add your own) for you to start creating an amazing list of guest experiences related to your chosen sporty theme:

Your 120 Seconds just started... GO!!!

The Arrival

Car park.

Staff. What are they wearing? (Referee's or umpire's outfit, swimming costume?)

Check-in desk. What do they say to you?

Key card. Shape, design?

Carpet.

Walls. Wallpaper design or pictures?

The lift.

The corridor.

The door to your room.

The Room

Carpet. Design?

Wallpaper. Design?

Ambience. Lights? Music?

Wardrobe.

Iron.

Kettle.

Fridge. What's in there?

Bed. Colours? Pillows?

Television. Is there a message? What does it say?

Bedside table. What's on there? (A scorecard?)

The Bathroom

Bathroom tiles.

Bathroom toiletries.

Shower/bath area.

Towels. (Are they in your favourite team colours, do they have a number on the back?)

The Food

Chefs and waiters. What are they wearing?

In-room menu. Name the dishes?

Breakfast menu. How it is served?

Evening meal and drinks.

The Departure

Check out. What is said to you?

How did you do? How many moments did you just create?

Now ask yourself the following crucial questions:

- If you were a guest staying at this hotel, would you return?
- Would you photograph or video any of these ideas and share them with the world via social media?
- Would you recommend this place to your family, friends and work colleagues?

If you answered yes to any of those then your ideas were worth sharing.

I hope that you have a great long list of ideas and that everyone contributed to the challenge. Of course now you can adopt this to your own business or organisation and conduct your very own 'from start to finish 120 Challenge'.

Of course not all of the ideas will work. Not all of them will be feasible. Heck, some of them may be illegal!!! But what you have done is opened up your eyes to what can be achieved in a very, very short space of time.

As you know all of my 120 Challenges are real. Turn to page 157 where I will reveal what I experienced from a themed hotel.

INTERVIEW

STEPHEN PAUL

MANAGING DIRECTOR

VALUED ACCOUNTANCY

Stephen is our accountant. Ask yourself this, would your accountant ever write the following line in an email to you? 'You have both done an awesome job and should be extremely proud.'

What is the greatest piece of service you've seen at Valued?

❝ So for the first two years of Valued we had Free Beer Friday at three o'clock and we'd invite staff and clients to come to talk to us about anything at all. Whether they were thinking about starting a business or they wanted a bit of advice, or they just wanted to network, then it was OK to turn up and we'd buy them a beer, listen, learn and laugh. Clients turned up, over and over again and it became more social. We offered great value on a Friday afternoon.

What is YOUR number one customer service superpower?

To me, it's personal. Every single client that I interact with, whether they pay me a thousand pounds a month or they pay me fifty quid a month or ten pounds a month. The money's irrelevant. It's personal.

What three things can any business or organisation do right now to create a greater Celebrity Service experience?

1. Actually listen to the customer. Shut up and listen because they will talk.

2. Treat all your customers differently.

   Not all of us want to be a multimillionaire. Maybe what I'd like is more time with my family? So stop treating me like a person that wants to be a multimillionaire. Stop trying to sell me stuff about being a multimillionaire, sell me something that helps me get more time with my family.

3. Be present.

   Find out what the customer wants and help them get whatever it is they need.

What examples can you share of how you or your team deliver a greater internal experience?

We don't have pointless meetings.

It's gotta be fun. If it's not fun then it's bloody hard work and if it's hard work you're not going to do it right.

The other thing that we do is we find out how each team member likes to be praised, how each one likes to be rewarded. Do they want to be rewarded with money or time with family or extra holidays or a hug?

To make it personal, we have created Life Moments at Valued, so that staff members can take time out to celebrate or complete their life moments, which can be anything from attending school plays, waiting in for the plumber, working from home, developing hobbies. Whatever it may be, we will support the team in exchange for efficient working practices with our clients. Without every member of the Valued team we wouldn't be able to deliver what we do, it's all about them and the culture of the business.

What infuriates you most about customer service or the lack of?

Systems. So much of this world is automated, there's so much of it just driven by computers now. And the reason it's all done is for efficiencies. It's all done to save money, to make money, to upsell and to cross-sell; there are so many systems out there that treat everybody exactly the same. Get rid of them!

If you had a magic wand what would you wave it over to instantly ensure a greater service is delivered?

At the start I had 20 clients I personally looked after. So those 20 clients used to get a phone call from me every Friday morning religiously asking, 'How are you doing?' The question wasn't 'What's happening with your business?', it was, 'How are *you* doing?' The responses have been the foundation of some great client relationships. I still do that to a certain degree. Not as much as I would like to… so that would be my magic wand that I would wave, to bring back those calls straight away.

If you had to place a customer service star along Hollywood Boulevard, whose name would be on it?

Lyndsey Robinson. I've never seen anyone care about the clients as much as Lyndsey, in every aspect. The only person she cares about is her client, genuinely. Whether it's a big client, a small client it's irrelevant as she helps our clients as much as she possibly can. She understands their goals, their ambitions, their drive. And she's done that for years, without realising just how great she is at it.

TEN OUT
OF TEN

Quite simply 10 great experience ideas to get your creative teeth into…

Top marks to the following companies who delivered the following Celebrity Service moments…

1. Memories that stick

As you depart your holiday cottage at Bosinver every child receives a free gift. They can choose their favourite fridge magnet design. Guess where they will put their souvenir when they return home? And I wonder how long it will stay there?

2. A drop-off pick-me-up

Leaving your baby or young child at a day nursery for the first time can be very emotional. Thankfully, nurseries can make a big difference to the parents at the gates on their first day.

A LITTLE GIFT FROM US TO YOU

Your child is very special and today they join our school.

They'll begin an exciting journey and to learn things that are cool.

We know it will be tearful, as you let your little one go.

Please trust us to look after them as we help them to play and grow.

So dry your tears and make a drink then enjoy a chocolate treat.

Because in just an hour or two, you'll be rushed back off your feet!

Love from Nursery XXX

3. It's a wrap

The team at Johnnie Johnson Housing didn't just hand out copies of the Celebrity Service book at Christmas, they ensured the paper design and the bow added to the gift experience.

4. Creativity covered

Some gifts are lovely, some are personalised, some are needed, and sometimes they are all three! Frasers Edinburgh showing their creativity once again.

5. A fitting end

We have waited for what seems like centuries for furniture manufacturers and suppliers to come up with a solution to the 'there's one screw missing' complaint. Thank you NEXT for fixing the problem.

SPARE PARTS FITTING

Just to let you know we have included a small quantity of fixings in case of mishap, so don't worry if you've got a few left when you've finished

6. Off your trolley

Throughout the year the team at MDL Marinas fill their amazing 'trolley of treats' and push it along the jetties to every boat owner. Handing out sweets and treats as they go. And when it's hot, they deliver free cold drinks and ice creams.

7. Curious George

At Cheval Three Quays, London you can borrow a soft and cuddly unicorn toy called George from reception. When you post your photographs of him onto their Facebook page you have the chance to not only win cuddly George but a goody bag too!

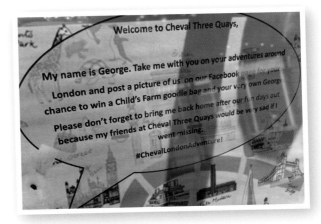

8. Digital to physical

Online personalised gifts or cards make a great impression on your clients, customers and suppliers. When you see both your name and the team come together for the photograph, it means a lot! Thank you for the thank you Sphere Digital Recruitment.

9. Sign of the times

In a world of instructions, directions and advice, Malmaison managed to spot the opportunity to make their guests smile.

10. License to celebrate

Morpeth based, Blackshaws Suzuki, made up special edition license plates as a thank you for my talk. They celebrated a century of business, and will no doubt celebrate another 100 years with moments like this.

LINDSAY SOUTHWARD

DIRECTOR OF PEOPLE AND BRAND DEVELOPMENT

VILLAGE HOTELS

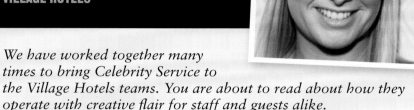

We have worked together many times to bring Celebrity Service to the Village Hotels teams. You are about to read about how they operate with creative flair for staff and guests alike.

What is the greatest piece of service you've seen at Village Hotels?

" My standout piece of service was at one of our hotels where I took my daughter on a weekend away. I think that most people in service or even just most mothers and fathers would say that if your kids are happy and looked after it makes a lasting impression on the whole guest experience for that family.

We went to stay at Cameron House in Scotland. My daughter would have been about five at the time and she carried this giant teddy bear dog around everywhere with her, along with another, more traditional teddy.

When we arrived, the concierge bent down to talk to Jessica and ask her name. She told him. And then he said, 'Who's this?' And she said, 'Well, this is Big Dog.' And then he said, 'And what's Teddy called?' And she said, 'Teddy, obviously!'

So she says, 'OK, great. You go off to walk around the lake and when your room's ready, we'll give you a call on your mobile number.' When the time came, they came out around the lake to pick us up, which was also lovely, but not something that was special as they do that for everybody. But as we got to the room and walked in, there on the bed were three teddies, Cameron House Hotel teddies. There was Jess's Big Dog and there was Jess's Teddy. Big Dog was dressed in its own Cameron House dressing gown, and Teddy had his own little dressing gown made out of a towel and with them there was a little note.

It said, 'Dear Jess, We thought that Big Dog and Teddy might be a bit lonely while you're on your walk. So we got them some friends. Lots of love from Cameron House.' This had quite an impact. They'd gone to this trouble and they'd remembered the teddies' names and Jessica's name. They made it feel like we were part of something.

What is YOUR number one customer service superpower?

I would say that my superpower is just being me, I suppose, and my energy. I think that's the one thing a lot of people often tell me, that's kind of my secret weapon, is that I just can't stop and I just keep going. This energy I have keeps other people going and it becomes infectious. When people are motivated to move things forward and get things done, they get fully engaged in projects. I think if you've got it, that's the power that you can use to influence a lot of things that happen in a business.

What is the greatest customer service experience you've ever received?

Teddy got left in Sainsbury's once. And obviously, as you already know, he's very, very important and very special to Jessica. Teddy was in the packing area with the bags, which was where he was left, and we walked home without Teddy. Realising, we turned to walk back, but even before we could get back to the store, the girl who was on the checkout had run out of the shop to follow Jessica with Teddy and met us halfway.

The Sainsbury's shop assistant could have just put it in lost property. She could have just given it to the customer service desk. She could have waited for us to come back. But instead she'd asked her supervisor if she could follow us. That didn't cost anything, it was just caring.

What three things can any business or organisation do right now to create a greater Celebrity Service experience?

1. Listen to your employees.

2. Engage with your employees on all levels.

3. Think outside the box to do something different. Don't do what you've always done just because you've always done it.

What examples can you share of how you or your team deliver a greater internal experience?

We introduced a people strategy to help with employee retention by improving communication to give people an understanding of who we are, what the brand is about and where we are going.

When people joined the company they would get this big wad of paper – a contract and starter letters and forms and all this information, which doesn't really engage them in the business. We looked at the psychology of engagement prior to somebody starting the role. What's important to them? On the day that they get offered the job what's important to them is to be excited about who they are going to work for. At this point they're not really bothered about what that disciplinary process is or how they book holidays. They just want to know what working for Village is going to look like.

We then looked at their experience of the days and weeks leading up to starting in a job. We looked at an induction in a pre-employment environment rather than everything happening on day one. To get them excited and engaged we offered them a gift from Village.

1. A scratch card and a reusable Starbucks cup.

   This isn't just any old reusable Starbucks cup (contributing to our sustainability project). Because we have Starbucks at Village Hotels they can get Starbucks at 50% off as a staff discount every day.

2. A get to know you letter.

   We asked them lots of questions in this letter, posing choices such as… Wine or beer? Night or day? Straight or curly? Movie or TV box sets? These random questions give us insights into people. For example, in answering the question 'Wine or beer?' someone might say 'Neither, I don't drink'. We know now that this person isn't motivated by getting a bottle of wine or a crate of beer as a reward. How often do you know that about four and a half thousand employees? So now we've got something personal about every single one of them. If we know that they'd like a Crunchie as opposed to a Snickers then they get a Crunchie on a Friday to just say thank you for what they've done.

3. A plant.
   This looks like a pre-packaged bit of soil and not much more. But when you cut off the top of this package, there are some seeds in it. We invite them to water the soil and the seeds and let it grow. It's a growing plant that is intended to mirror their own development within their Village journey.

   It's not a huge expense, but it's something that's branded. It's personal. And we send it all in the post. You don't get stuff in the post anymore. Everybody gets stuff online and it gets lost. It's an email or a discount code for this or that. But because you got it in the post, it becomes quite significant because somebody knocked at the door and you got a parcel that you weren't expecting. So it gives a sense of being valued and that you're going to be part of something that's a little bit different.

What infuriates you most about customer service or the lack of?

I think it's frustrating when people don't see that it's really simple to get customer loyalty. If you just genuinely care then you can really enjoy what you do. It frustrates me that if you don't enjoy it, you don't need to do it. If you don't want to smile every day and you don't want to pretend you're happy, then you should go do something else.

If you had a magic wand what would you wave it over to instantly ensure a greater service is delivered?

I'd probably like to wave the wand so everyone would understand what Celebrity Service is. It's not about spending money, it's seeing that Celebrity Service doesn't have to be a big grand gesture. I would wave that wand over probably the entire hospitality industry so we could all see what the difference is – doing all of those customer service things that you've always done but doing them a little bit differently. And doing them with absolute sincere, genuine care, not doing them because your job description says that you should.

If you had to place a customer service star along Hollywood Boulevard, whose name would be on it?

Josie Simcox, who is our general manager at Village, Farnborough.

She is one of those people who tirelessly thinks about two things: her guests and her people. These two are always, always top of her list. If I send out a people initiative or an idea, she's already thought about it. Every single story about guests that Josie tells is about creating an individual experience. Like a lot of people at Village, she's got this tireless energy and enthusiasm to just be happy and create a culture that people want to thrive in.

DREAM
TEAMS

What does it look like when an entire team comes together to create memorable experiences. Here are a couple of my favourites…

Houston, we have a solution!

I swapped the Cowboys for the Texans, as I made the short hop from Dallas to Houston, to work alongside Samantha Elliott and Jon Lanclos and their team at PCH (Preferred Corporate Housing).

PCH provide luxurious extended-stay lodgings throughout the United States. Helping to relocate employees and their families, they pride themselves on creating home-from-home furnished properties covering over 75,000 destinations in all 50 states. But here's the thing… this service is mainly provided via telephone or email with the HR department of the corporation concerned. In fact, they rarely have the opportunity to meet the individuals or families face to face.

Jumping in an Uber I arranged a detour via the NRG stadium to grab a quick selfie and to pick up a replica miniature helmet.

No helmet.

No helmets in the stock room.

Not even an offer of a secret tour.

Not to worry, there is always Amazon when I return back to the UK.

The following day I worked with the entire PCH team, and boy what a bunch! They were easily one of the friendliest, warmest and most welcoming teams I have had the pleasure to spend time with. While the Houston sun was blazing outside, inside we had lift-off with ideas soaring like rockets.

The morning session was over and then to lunch, where three things happened:

1. We had lunch.

2. We topped up our Vitamin D outside with a group photograph.

3. A few folk must have thought they were appearing on the hit TV show *Supermarket Sweep* as they spent their break dashing about to find a variety of items. Gathering around me, they presented their trolley haul (as a thank you for my talk so far).

Inside a brand new Astros sports bag was an array of sporting Houston goodies. And guess what… right there at the bottom of the goodie bag was a Houston Texans t-shirt and a miniature Texans helmet! (I had briefly mentioned to Samantha and Jon the night before that I loved the game and was hoping to pick up a helmet at the airport before I left.) Wow!

Of course it is not just me who's been on the receiving end of Celebrity Service thanks to PCH. They have been delivering it since they started in 1996. Here are some of my favourite stories.

'One of the charities we support with our award-winning 'Preferred Charity Helpers' program is an organisation called the Amschwand Sarcoma Foundation. Preferred Corporate Housing provides furnished apartments for patients receiving support from this foundation while they are undergoing cancer treatment in the Houston Medical Center. The PCH team wanted to bring a little holiday cheer for these patients during Christmas time, so they snuck into each apartment to deliver and decorate a Christmas tree for each one.

'We took your advice, Geoff, and decided to personalise a birthday message for one of our clients who we had been struggling to create a personal connection with. Her account team created a video message for her and sent her flowers. She absolutely loved it and it

helped us build a nice foundation with her! She posted her thanks all over social media!

'We found out that one of our client's birthdays was coming up and she had previously mentioned how much she loves this particular hole-in-the-wall bar near her office. Our team surprised her with an impromptu party there, complete with her favourite drink already poured when she came in. She was thrilled that we had paid attention.

'Since most of our communication with our clients happens via phone and email, we aren't often face to face with them and sometimes struggle to keep the communication personalised. We quickly realised that when people see our faces, they realise we are real, caring people who want to help them, not just some faceless names behind email addresses. We started putting together photos of our account teams to send to our clients when they sign on with us (along with some useful PCH swag). This way they can put our photo in their office and hopefully make human connections with us as we work together. We've even had a few clients send us their own family photos back for us to keep at our desks!

What Samantha and Jon have created is a culture of hard work, fun and passion that creates the ideas to engage and delight the people they never meet. It is said that the family that plays together, stays together. I have the pleasure of knowing a lot of the team via social media and they are one of the tightest knit groups who all play and work hard together. And the results show.

An injection of fun

I spent two amazing weeks in Australia delivering Celebrity Service across six cities as part of the AFA Roadshow. Kicking off in Hobart, Tasmania, we hopped across to Adelaide, on to Perth, back across to Melbourne, up to Brisbane and then swooping into the finale to be held in Sydney. The series of events was easily one of the best tours I have ever been involved in. We were a band of brothers and sisters who laughed, worked hard, laughed some more, encouraged one another from the outset. And then laughed some more.

Outside the main rooms where the speakers did their stuff, in the foyer, the exhibitors gathered to display their wares to potential clients. One of these, Sunsuper, stood out like a beacon. While every exhibitor had their own piece of marketing to attract everyone's attention (mainly sweets, cupcakes or memory sticks) Sunsuper did something a little different.

They are renowned for supplying doughnuts on their exhibition stands for delegates to enjoy. In every city they call ahead and place an order with a local bakery to supply hundreds of fresh doughnuts on the morning of the event. However, it was when we reached Melbourne that a great customer service idea came face to face with a greater customer experience. As I walked past the stands I was stopped in my tracks by what caught my eyes inside the doughnut boxes. Sunsuper chose Bistro Morgan to deliver their treats. And this is what arrived!!!

By adding a syringe filled with jam, chocolate or caramel, Bistro Morgan created a brilliant customer experience. They took a normal product, a product we all know and love, and added a twist on the experience. I am often asked what makes a memorable event. I'd naturally say the speakers and content first, but then the audience, the venue, the theme – they all play important roles. Yet it is always those little creative touches that can get us talking, snapping and sharing.

What twist can you add to your products right now to create a Bistro Morgan style experience? Why not get in touch and let me know?

INTERVIEW

JULIE CHEESMAN

BRAND OPERATIONS DIRECTOR

voco™ HOTELS

Julie and I have worked together many times and she has led a fantastic team to achieve amazing growth of this exciting brand.

What is the greatest piece of service you've seen at voco™ Hotels?

"I like to think that we inspire people to treat customers like they would like to be treated themselves. I'm always thinking about how you can go that one step further. I think it's really important that we remember in hospitality we have the ability to create an experience and a memory for someone. So we really need to think about what that entails.

One example I've seen recently is Ivy at voco™ Oxford Thames. She picked up from the reservation notes that the visiting guests were staying at the hotel to celebrate the 70th birthday of their father, Dom, who was partially sighted. Ivy purchased a braille embossing kit so that she could deliver a personalised card for Dom to remind him of his special birthday at the hotel.

Everybody thinks that giving people great service and memories involves throwing money at everything but it's just so simple what we're asking people to do. We just need to make sure that the leaders of the business, whether it's a hotel or a department store or any business, are completely empowering their people to make those decisions. To enable them to do those things, to deliver that experience for that individual and to put themselves in the customer's shoes and think what would make this a memorable experience for them?

What is YOUR number one customer service superpower?

I tend to blow the trumpet of individuals around me as opposed to my own. You're only as successful as the people around you. I've had a lot of people say to me, 'Do you own a yellow cape, Julie? You're a bit like Wonder Woman?' I suppose I am a little bit Wonder Woman-like and when I'm faced with a challenge I am usually right in the middle of it, but I am also the one that is keen to help and guide everybody out of it. I will always try to get over or ahead of a challenge, or try to solve it with others. As I don't have all the answers the best ideas often come from within the team you are working with. Most importantly, I am always keen to learn from it so it doesn't happen again.

I also say it's not about me, it's not about what I know, it's about who I know. It's about my network within the organisation and outside of that organisation. It's about knowing who to go to and remembering that you are not expected to know everything yourself. This is one of the things that I try to instil in the people that work for me. It's not about conquering the world on your own, it's about teamwork. This is about pulling on the skills and knowledge of people around you in order for everyone to shine together.

What is the greatest customer service experience you've ever received?

I bought a car recently. So I think that they got this really right in terms of gaining a lifetime of loyalty. But it wasn't a 'they', it was one particular person.

Davinder was the salesman I met and struck the deal with. When I went to collect my car I was made to feel so special. Like the Queen. It was more than just a bunch of flowers, set of mugs, all the free stuff. There was this whole unexpected reveal, a blowing of trumpets when the black cover came off the new car, a personalised sign next to the car. I mean, it cost absolutely nothing for them to do that. But it was just so special and made me feel so valued.

Even after the sale when I went in for a service and Davinder walked past me he took the time to stop and say, 'Hi, how are you?' and we had a chat. You know, he's just someone for me who is just an all-time superstar; he's really connected to his clients.

What three things can any business or organisation do right now to create a greater Celebrity Service experience?

1. Stay connected. In times of hardship people remember how they were treated and how you make them feel.

2. Remembering that creating memories and guest experiences don't always cost you lots of money. You don't need to over-think it. Do what you think is right, go with your gut and those little things will have the biggest impact.

3. Make sure you share examples of your Celebrity Service. So whether that be on an individual level, whether that be on a team level through social platforms, recognise what people are doing. Talk about it, video it, post it, share it. Behaviour breeds behaviour.

What infuriates you most about customer service or the lack of?

Making a promise and not keeping it, letting people down.

If you had a magic wand what would you wave it over to instantly ensure a greater service is delivered?

The one key point of difference that we have across many industries is our people. So my wand would like to give every one of those people, alongside accountability and responsibility, the motivation, energy and passion to deliver magical memories.

THE BIG
REVEALS

You have created some amazing ideas with the 120 Challenge. Now take a look at the experiences that inspired those challenges...

The Cellar Door

Remember The Elephant House? (See page 62)

All of my 120 Challenges are real, they are not made up.

Opposite The Elephant House is a place called The Cellar Door. As Hayley and I walked across the road we noticed that they too had decided to create an experience to put a smile on their customers' faces.

Even if you seem to be in the shadow of a competitor, always look at ways to create a great customer experience. Even if it's the words you use on a piece of paper, you never know when someone might take a picture, mention you in their talks. One day they may even write about you in their book.

You always have a choice. Embrace creativity and wave a magic wand over your business. And use the 120 Challenge with your own team to create a greater Celebrity Service experience at any given touchpoint.

Hotel Football

I was booked to open the Royal Bank of Scotland staff conference. Their annual event that year was in Manchester. Due to being onstage first thing the next morning I travelled down the night before so I could be ready for kick off. As luck would have it the venue for the conference was also the hotel I was staying in. Its name: Hotel Football.

It was the only time I hadn't googled a hotel before arriving. Knowing that this was a themed hotel I didn't want any spoilers.

The hotel was great. Contemporary in design and the staff were friendly and welcoming. The first thing I noticed before I checked in were the pictures on the walls, which happened to feature one of my favourite movies. I was given my key card and off I went to my room overlooking Old Trafford Football Stadium, home to Manchester United.

The wallpaper was very dark, almost black. On moving closer you could see the pattern was of old Paninni football stickers. The room was spacious and bright and when I opened the fridge it was stocked with Vimto drinks and sweets (the company is Manchester based).

All in all an excellent experience, an excellent stay and an excellent conference.

But would I have changed anything? Possibly. Two ideas sprung to mind during my stay.

The first popped into my head during check in. It was the key card that led me to it. It was blank. It was white. Oh, I thought... this could be an amazing opportunity. A chance to deliver something very quirky and different.

Guest arrives at reception to check in...

Receptionist: Is this your first time at Hotel Football?

Guest: Yes.

Receptionist (brandishing a yellow key card): Okay first offence. Here are the rules, your room is (give directions) breakfast is from (give the times) your wifi code is... And if you need anything at all call over to the bench by phoning down.

(Of course all this is done with a big smile, treating the guest to a fun experience they've never had before.)

Or...

Guest arrives at reception to check in...

Receptionist: Is this your first time at Hotel Football?

Guest: No, I've been before.

Receptionist (handing guest a red key card): We've told you before... you know where the rooms are, you know the wifi, now off to your room.

Also delivered with a smile this could become a great talking point for each and every guest.

Harry Potter

was

(Probably)

written

here too...

(Maybe?)

ESCAPE TO VICTORY

EAT
SLEEP

The second idea that came to me was when I opened the drawer under the television and found the hairdryer. Now based on where we were (just metres from Old Trafford) I knew we could have been just one word away from creating a greater experience.

The famous Sir Alex Ferguson, one of the greatest managers to have ever graced the game won every trophy going while at Manchester United. A popular story about him is that if his team were not playing so well, at half-time he would give them the legendary 'hairdryer treatment' – he would shout at the players so hard their hair would be blown back.

The word I would have embroidered onto the bag underneath the word 'hairdryer' in very small letters would have been treatment. Most fans visiting the hotel would recognise this and I'd imagine it would put a huge smile on their face.

Back to the 120 Challenge, the greatest answer I ever heard and the one that brought the entire house down was a gentleman who stood up and said:

'Our team would install mattresses on the beds with special motion sensors. When any bed reached a certain amount of bounce/movement, this would trigger the sensors and out of the ceiling speakers would be heard a commentator shouting GOAL!!!!!!!!!!!!!!!!!!!!!!!!'

AND THE WINNERS ARE...

Those who embrace Celebrity Service into their culture, quite simply, win. But what do I mean by winning? It's certainly not the same for everyone, but the constant stream of results I hear and read from all sectors and brands makes me extremely proud.

Let me leave you with a handful of some of these amazing results...

Increased Net Promoter Score (NPS)

If you are looking to increase your NPS (and who wouldn't?) this was an incredible message I received from high street brand leader, Tesco Mobile. They informed me their NPS had risen an incredible 1.8 within just weeks of our first event together.

Increased awards

'Geoff Ramm, you are a star. Over the last two years we have been applying Celebrity Service in our business to ensure we meet and exceed our guests' expectations (humans and four-legged friends) and on Thursday evening we scooped three Gold Awards in the Devon Tourism Awards held at Highbullen Hotel.

'Thank you for your support and friendship over the last few years. Celebrity Service has had a big impact on our business. Keep doing what you are doing, it's making a real difference to people and businesses all over the world.'

Bob Boothby, Millbrook Cottages & Estate

Increased scores

After the inspiring session delivered by Geoff each hotel established a clear plan of action around Celebrity Service. They could challenge themselves to deliver fabulous hosted Celebrity Service and enter into the voco™ service millionaires challenge, all of which resulted in an uplift of guest experience scores across all the open and operating UK and Ireland voco™ hotels.

Increased sales

'Dear Geoff,

'I just wanted to get in touch to say that yesterday I was trying to sell a caravan to a man who was based in Yorkshire. I was up here in Scotland. Whilst trying to explain the pitch I had a flash of inspiration following your session at the BH&HPA Conference in Edinburgh.

'I went outside and took a video of the caravan pitch and sent the personalised video to him.

'A £43,000 van was sold within 1 hour!'

Elspeth Sutton, General Manager, Cally Estate

'I've attended more conferences than I care to remember over the last quarter of a century working in recruitment. Your presentation is certainly one of the most engaging, but definitely has the most instantly useable techniques.

'You asked for feedback, here it is…

'Rather than the usual 'booking managers' we decided that we should seek out some of the unsung heroes amongst our customers: folks who process our invoices, issue PO numbers, have HR or training responsibilities, etc.

'We took thank you cards and chocolates to every existing client with it being Valentine's this week. We have had an overwhelming response, and met face to face with what turned out to be some of the most important people in our customers' organisations. None of these people are decision makers, although all of them are significant decision influencers. As a result of a simple thank you card and a box of chocolates we were told by one decision maker that they are now going to book all warehouse staff through us.

'I estimate c£50K additional spend. Thank you for the inspiration.'

Tony Goacher, Driver Hire Recruitment

Increased morale

'Just thought I'd let you know you inspired us this last week or two with your "Welcome Back" videos. You posed the question, "How will you welcome back your customers?" Well it sparked the question, "How will we welcome back our internal customers?" too.

'Then we started talking about unfurloughing and listened to the team to hear they were nervous, apprehensive and worried about returning... not about the virus but about fitting back in to the retained team. They said it was like the first day in a new job or at school! Wow! So we reminded them that they are stars... celebrities.

'We created special personalised posters on the door as this would be the first thing they see. And the stars were made from words their colleagues use to describe them. It's been picked up by the Specsavers group and we've attributed it back to your work! The result is a buzzing happy team.'

Brad Parkes, FBDO C/L, Director Specsavers Solihull

Increased ideas

Throughout the Superstars interviews I asked everyone 'What is your number one superpower?'

If I were to ask myself the very same question I would probably answer 'The ability to instantly come up with ideas'. Whether I am faced with a question or challenge onstage, onscreen or in a meeting, it's just one of those abilities that comes most naturally to me.

The irony of coming up with the idea of the 120 Challenge to inspire ideas is not lost.

Of course ideas will remain ideas unless action is taken. And when action is taken, the results will light up your business and excite your customers.

Handing it to them

I set my alarm for 3:30 am and at 4:00 am I delivered a virtual live event across Australia. One hour of Celebrity Service to the Mobile Skips franchisees who provide clever solutions to a growing worldwide waste problem. Jacob Spencer is the Managing Director and despite them having fantastic online reviews and being highly recommended by their customers, he wanted to introduce the concept to everyone to further improve their customer experience.

In 60 minutes I shared many stories and ideas and two of them really stuck with Mobile Skips.

Firstly, one of my favourites, which is 'instant personalised video messages'. The franchisees record a message on their mobile phone and email it to the customer, mentioning the customer's name, introducing themselves, announcing what time they would be arriving and, as a result, putting a human touch to the delivery touchpoint.

Secondly, my idea was 'to provide gloves for every customer', not just any old glove, something of real quality that would last for many years. When the skip is left on the customer's driveway and filled with garden and home waste (it's a messy job), a pair of gloves would come in handy. Ideally, the gloves would be branded to serve as a promotional reminder whenever the customer wore them long after the skip had left, for jobs around the home or garden.

Jacob and the team loved this idea too and so they took it one stage further and added a handwritten, personalised note to go with every pair of gloves.

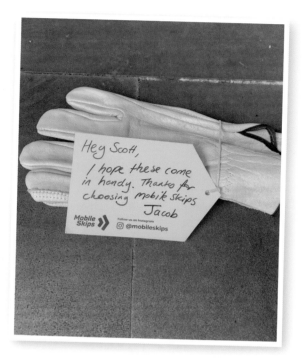

Put yourself in the customer's shoes. You order a skip, you receive a personalised message, and you now have a pair of gloves to keep your hands safe and clean. Two touchpoints transformed with Superstar ideas.

Calculating cuppas

On page 130 of this book you will find an interview with Stephen Paul. Twice a year, Hayley and I venture up to his office in Consett, County Durham, to either plan the year ahead or to finalise our year end accounts.

We are always welcomed with a big smile, a handshake or even a hug. Stephen's first question is always 'Would you like a tea or coffee?' We make our choice and within five minutes our tea or coffee arrives in a mug or cup. This is good service, good coffee, good tea, everything is good. But could it be better? Everything can be better. We just need to pause, observe and look to add a sprinkle of Celebrity Service to the experience.

At the end of one of our meetings Stephen asked for my advice and ideas. 'I'd like to inject some Celebrity Service into the first impressions when clients enter our office. Have you any ideas Geoff?'

I had one. Quick as a flash I mentioned the tea and coffee, or to be more precise the mugs and cups the drinks arrived in. There was nothing wrong with them, they were just a little out of sync. I'd noticed that they were different colours, shapes and sizes. On one occasion I was given a coffee in a Newcastle United mug! (I've never tasted such bitter coffee in all my days.) Of course we are there for the great advice not the carrier of hot liquids, but it's the smallest of details which can cause the biggest waves of delight.

When I mentioned the mugs and cups were out of sync and did not match his brand, Stephen's lightbulb moment had arrived and he immediately mentioned sourcing branded mugs with the 'Valued' logo on the side.

A great idea. But can you go even further? Always.

You see when you know a client or potential client has made an appointment to see you, you also know when they are arriving and most importantly you also know their name. So use this basic information you have and create some magic.

Picture the scene, you enter your accountant's (or future accountant's) office, you receive a big smile, handshake, (hugs optional) and you are offered a tea or coffee.

Five minutes later your hot drink arrives…. It's in a lovely professional branded mug but on the other side *is your name*!

Stephen and the team now create this for every existing and potential client, who take their mugs away with them back to their own offices for all to see.

Do you think they love it? Do you think they are amazed at the length the team have gone to make them feel special?

If you had a meeting with three potential accountants who offer similar services and pricing but one of them did this, who would you be more inclined to choose?

We've all heard the phrase 'good to great' but there is another level, and it's called Celebrity Service.

So let's bypass striving for 'great' and go direct to Superstar status.

Achieving increased scores is one thing, but the team at voco™ Oxford Thames created a moment of magic one customer and his family will never forget. It was Don's birthday and his family had called to book a table in the restaurant at voco on his birthday. During the phone call, his family had informed the hotel staff that Don was partially sighted. The voco™ team wanted to give Don a birthday card when he arrived but they also had an amazing idea. They sourced a braille machine and created a moment of pure magic – a birthday card personalised with a braille message from the voco™ team.

Sometimes you see the difference, sometimes you smell the difference and sometimes you can just feel the difference a team will go to in order to create Celebrity Service.

So you have read the amazing stories. You have taken on board the ideas. You are now preparing your first set of 120 Challenges for your team.

And more importantly you can see what makes a Superstar in the world of Celebrity Service. I want to personally wish you every success.

Whatever results you go on to achieve with your team, brand or organisation, please let me know which of the stories have inspired you and the changes you have made. I'd love to hear from you, so do message me at geoff@geofframm.com

To the people and businesses featured in this book, thank you. Thank you for spotting the opportunities. Thank you for taking action. Thank you for making a difference. Thank you for being true Celebrity Service Superstars. Your dedication to delivering a greater customer experience will never go unnoticed.

Before I bid you farewell here are just a few things to think about before you close this book...

If you are not being talked about, then you are not delivering an experience that deserves to be talked about.

No matter how well you are performing there is always a gap. You now know how to fill the gap. Life is too short. Start today.

Take care and best wishes.

Geoff